In Defence of Classical Music

By the same author

Books

Illegal Harmonies: Music in the 20th century
Undue Noise: Words about music
Composer to Composer: Conversations about contemporary music
Speaking in Tongues: The songs of Van Morrison (with Martin
    Buzacott)

Music on CD

Whispers (Tall Poppies TP053)
Harbour (TP128)
Icarus (TP150)

In Defence of Classical Music

ANDREW FORD

ABC
Books

First published by ABC Books for the
AUSTRALIAN BROADCASTING CORPORATION
GPO Box 9994 Sydney NSW 2001

Copyright © Andrew Ford 2005

First published in September 2005
Reprinted June 2006

ISBN 10: 0 7333 1594 1
ISBN 13: 978 0 7333 1594 7

Cover and internal design by Chrisabella Designs
Cover image by Getty Images
Author photo by Jim Rolon
Internals set in 11/17pt Weiss by Kirby Jones
Colour reproduction by Pageset, Victoria
Printed and bound by Quality Printing, Hong Kong, China

6 5 4 3 2

To the unknown listener

Contents

Preface

(including a note to the pedants)

A few years ago in a junk shop in the New South Wales Southern Highlands I came across a little book — even smaller than this — entitled *Musical Taste and How to Form It*. It was published in 1925, and its author was M. D. Calvocoressi. When I found it, I was thinking a lot about the issues outlined in the pages that follow; indeed, the book itself was already planned and commissioned. It seemed to me that Calvocoressi's primer would come in useful. Plainly, it was going to be full of old-fashioned patrician nonsense — after all, you can't tell someone how to form their musical taste — and so I would make fun of it, perhaps in my foreword, like an after-dinner speaker warming up with a few preliminary jokes before going on to put everything to rights in the main body of my book.

Michel-Dimitri Calvocoressi (1877–1944) was a French-born music critic of Greek parentage, writing in English and active in Britain. His book was not what I was expecting. With a mixture of surprise and mild disappointment, I found myself agreeing with nearly everything the author advocated. He began his volume by asking why anyone should want to read it, and he was evidently aware of the paradox of setting out to help others form their tastes. But he also knew, and was at pains to demonstrate, that there is more to classical music than pretty sounds or stirring tunes. You may, in the first place, be attracted to a piece by Beethoven or Sibelius or John Adams by 'the noise it makes' (to borrow a remark from the conductor Thomas Beecham), and you may well choose to leave it at that. Liking the noise can certainly be enough. But, as with any great art, if you dig deeper, you will always find more. Calvocoressi's book aimed to offer help with this, and so does the present book.

Besides *Musical Taste and How to Form It*, Calvocoressi wrote volumes devoted to the music of Schumann, Liszt, Glinka and Musorgsky. He was a personal friend of Maurice Ravel. Some of his poems were set to music by Albert Roussel, he had an early association with Diaghilev's Ballets Russes, and he lived long enough to translate into English the libretto of Shostakovich's opera *The Lady Macbeth of the Mtsensk District*. In other words, he knew classical music to be a living and continuously evolving tradition. Yet if he could have read my previous sentence, I think he would have raised an eyebrow at one word. You will notice that unlike the title of the book you are holding, Calvocoressi's title does not include the qualifier 'classical'. Before going any further, and in an effort to discourage a tedious correspondence with my more punctilious readers, let me first address my use of this word.

To describe the music of John Dowland or Kaija Saariaho — let alone both of them — as 'classical' is literal nonsense. I know that. Classical music, strictly speaking, was that composed in the last quarter of the eighteenth century and the first quarter of the nineteenth, a period dominated, at least from our perspective, by Haydn, Mozart and Beethoven. It was a time of balanced proportions and reasoned argument, in music as in all else — an antidote to the high drama of the baroque and self-regarding Romanticism which came either side of it. But the term 'classical music' (with a lower-case c) is how most people commonly refer to an entire Western tradition of notated music stretching roughly from the twelfth century to the present day. I suppose a more accurate term might be 'Western art music', but that is cumbersome. So in this book I use the word 'classical' instead, and, when I really do mean the music of Haydn, Mozart and Beethoven, I use the capital C.

Back to Calvocoressi. The reason he might have been surprised by the word 'classical' is that he would almost certainly have assumed that 'Western art music' was the subject of any book purporting to be about music. Calvocoressi was a music critic, not a classical music critic. There was no other sort of music critic in 1925. Today when one picks up a newspaper or a general-interest magazine and sees a section headed 'music', it will probably be about popular music. If there is anything at all about classical music in the same newspaper or magazine, it will be under the heading 'classical', generally at the bottom of the page, and certainly afforded fewer column inches.

If our mainstream journals are distinguishing between 'music' and 'classical', this alone should alert us to the fact that things have changed rather radically since Calvocoressi's day. Classical music is no longer mainstream. It hardly features in the popular media, you will encounter it very rarely on television (and only if you are an insomniac or at a loose end on a Saturday or Sunday afternoon) and it is not taught as part of the general curriculum in most of our schools — at least not in most of our public schools. You begin, perhaps, to see why today classical music can be made to seem like the pastime of an elite.

It is not the music's fault. Beethoven's symphonies and string quartets have not changed. People's need for musical nourishment has certainly not changed, unless it has become greater. What has changed, in the eighty years since the publication of *Musical Taste and How to Form It*, is public life. Politics, business and the mass media are interdependent as never before, and at the top of all these professions are men (and a few women) whose only real interest is the making of money. If you are one of these people, you have picked up this book by mistake. Put it down now because it will only make you cross. However, if you are not one of them, I hope you will find the following pages thought-provoking and enjoyable. Most of all, I hope you will go and listen to some of the pieces of music that are mentioned. I hope you will hear music you have never heard before, and I hope you will notice some new things in the music you already knew.

This book is in three parts. The first presents an argument. In essence, it is this: we live in a world in which it is increasingly hard to know what or whom to believe. For example, I no longer believe a word that any politician utters, particularly any politician in power. An admittedly small part of the lies we are fed insists that classical music is not for ordinary folk, but only for some imaginary 'elite'. This is not true. Classical music is for anyone who is interested, and it is of more value today than it has ever been, not least because it offers a powerful antidote to the liars.

The second part of the book consists of what I might call exemplars, ten of them. Each short essay takes as its starting point the music of a single composer. These are not intended as the ten greatest or most important composers in history (Bach, Mozart and Wagner are not among them), and neither are they my ten favourite composers. In electing to write about their music, I was hoping to present a composite picture of what classical music is, what it is capable of, (to some extent) how it works, and how it differs from other sorts of music.

The final section of the book, Making Notes, is the shortest and it contains three articles about my own music. This was part of my original plan for the book, but I will confess here that I changed my mind, back and forth, about including it, because it strikes me, at one level, as both self-important and presumptuous (and obviously if I think that, others will too). The original reason for putting it there was to allow me to speak to readers who are not themselves composers about what goes on in a composer's mind. I can't begin to tell you what Haydn or Brahms was thinking as he composed — that would be even more presumptuous — but I can tell you exactly what I was thinking. This is not the same as telling you what my music 'means' — I don't know the answer to that any more than I know what Haydn's or Brahms's music 'means' — but I can tell you some of what I was setting out to achieve. By extension, I hope it will become apparent how a composer thinks about matters of sound, structure and, sometimes, style.

Now, briefly, to business. Many of the ideas in Part One — and not a few of the actual words — were first tried out in public talks. I would like to express my appreciation to anyone who sat through these, and especially to those who asked questions or challenged my woollier thinking. In particular, those present at the annual address to the Music Council of Australia in 2003, at Adelaide Writers' Week in March 2004 and at a lecture at the Queensland Conservatorium of Music in October 2004 will probably recognise some of the writing. An edited version of the MCA address also appeared in the *Australian Financial Review*.

That same newspaper published the original versions of nine of the ten essays in Part Two, and I am particularly grateful to Hugh Lamberton for commissioning them. The *Fin*'s Friday Review section seems to me to be the last place in Australia's mainstream print media where you can read a long article about classical music. All these essays have been revised and in some cases expanded since their initial publication. The essay about Brahms is completely new. In Part Three, the section about *The Waltz Book* also first appeared in the *Australian Financial Review*, while some of the words about 'Blue Poles' in the section on *Manhattan Epiphanies* were originally written for an article in the *Sydney Morning Herald*.

I am grateful to Rodney Hall for permission to quote the lines from his libretto to *Whispers*, and to Thomas Shapcott for permission to reprint his poem 'Brahms'. W. H. Auden's poem

'The Composer' is published by Faber and Faber, and the extract is likewise used with permission.

Jacqueline Kent commissioned *In Defence of Classical Music*, left ABC Books in order to write her own book, and reappeared just in time to edit this volume. Working with her is always a pleasure. In Jacquie's absence, Jo Mackay saw the book through to its final stages. Thanks to them both.

Finally, I want to thank my wife, Anni Heino, who read most of these words first, and whose comments and suggestions unfailingly resulted in improvements. Any remaining errors of judgment or fact are probably there because I failed fully to heed her advice.

Andrew Ford
March 2005

PART ONE

*In Defence of
Classical Music*

Killing the clichés

It might surprise some people to learn that, at the start of the twenty-first century, classical music needs defending. In a way, it surprises me too. This music and the tradition to which it belongs strike me as possibly of more use to us today than ever before, and so it seems odd that their future should be threatened. The first part of this book considers why classical music is under threat and how this came about, and it attempts to explain why a tradition of written-down music is vital to our society's wellbeing, and why we need to protect it.

We often hear the cliché that classical music needs to make itself more 'accessible'. It is always hard to know what is meant by this. As with so many other clichés, it probably means nothing very specific. But take it, for a moment, at face value. For music to be accessible, it must allow the listener access, a way in: to use a rather more old-fashioned but more precise term, the listener must be able to appreciate it. On that basis, I would contend that there is nothing inherently inaccessible about classical music, or any other sort of music. If you present a piece of music to an audience it is hard to see how you might be barring it from access. Of course, some things take more time to appreciate than others, but that is another matter.

If an inexperienced listener finds the idea of classical music somehow intimidating, which is what the cliché seems to imply, this is, I suggest, because of the vast amount of rubbish talked about the subject, mostly by people who overuse words such as 'accessible'. This sort of lazy thinking takes hold with great ease in our modern world; indeed it is encouraged, every day, by a tabloid media. In order to help us spot some of the laziest thinking, I have made a list of ten more clichés about classical music, all of which, I imagine, will be familiar. A few of these are ostensibly positive, the others are clearly negative, and all of them are untrue. The first two are related.

1. *You need a special education to understand classical music.*

2. *With classical music, you should just lie back and let it wash over you.*
Neither of these statements is accurate, and it is hard to know which is more unhelpful to the uninitiated. The response to the first myth is simple: you don't need a special education; anyone at any time can appreciate classical music, just by listening to it. Oddly enough, that is also the response to the second myth: if you want to get anything out of music, there

is no point in lying back in the hope that something will happen; you will have to listen to it. As with any worthwhile music, listening is active, not passive. Classical music will not do all the work for you. Because it is generally rather detailed and often involves a musical argument being advanced over a stretch of time longer than that of the average piece of music, classical music only does about half the work. The composer writes the music, often over a period of weeks, months or sometimes years, but the audience brings its ears, its concentration, its imagination and its memory to the piece. The listener enters into a partnership with the music.

3. *People who like classical music are snobs.*

Well some of them are. There are also folk-music snobs and techno snobs and blues snobs and, God knows, jazz snobs. It is human nature to believe that the things you like are the best. And yet snobbishness suggests exclusivity, while most music fans are anything but exclusive. In truth they are far more likely to be cultural imperialists, seeking to persuade others of the central importance of Wagner or John Coltrane, or of the genuine merits of the latest synthetic pop star invented by business executives to relieve children of their pocket money. Cultural imperialism has gained a poor reputation over the last century, but even at its subjugating worst imperialism often involved an element of generosity. However misguided they might be, imperialists generally feel they are improving the lives of the people they are telling what to do. Introducing someone to Wagner is the act of a missionary, not of a snob.

4. Classical music, especially Mozart, will make you more intelligent.

Apparently, if you play a recording of Mozart's D major sonata for two pianos to laboratory rats, it helps them find their way around a maze. If you play the same piece to students, they concentrate a little better, though the effect seems to wear off. I think it wears off with the rats too. Presumably the effect is created not only by this piece, which in any case is not Mozart's very greatest work (or even his greatest sonata). But it prompts a series of questions. Is the perceived rise in powers of concentration and (in the case of the rats) spatial awareness to do with (a) Mozart, (b) the sound of the piano, or (c) the key of D major? What about tempo? Is a slow performance better than a fast one? And is one recording more effective than another? Do Murray Perahia and Radu Lupu help rats and students more or less than András Schiff and Peter Serkin? And would a live performance be more effective than a CD? And what if that performance contained some wrong notes: would 10 per cent wrong notes result in only 90 per cent of the normal increase in spatial awareness? And do you get more from it if you really concentrate, as opposed to having the music playing in the background? And are rats really capable of musical appreciation anyway? Let us move on.

5. Listening to classical music will make you a better human being.

This is a particularly insidious myth, but fortunately an easy one to dispel. Here is how you do it. Write a list of all those composers from history who were drunks, drug addicts, lechers, liars, debtors, grasping ingrates, appalling paranoid whingers or insufferably arrogant pricks. Now cross their names off the list of all the composers who have ever lived. You will find you are left with the Abbess Hildegard of Bingen and perhaps three or four others. If classical music is composed by reprobates of that order, why should it be morally improving to listen to it?

One hears the same view expressed in relation to literature and the other arts. It seems to be a version of the Protestant work ethic. Because *War and Peace* is harder to read than a Jeffrey Archer novel, it is believed by some people to make you into a better person. I suppose reading Tolstoy might improve your powers of concentration and your memory, particularly for long Russian names, but it will not do anything for your morals, and neither will a preference for Sibelius over silverchair. On the contrary, if art affected your morals at all it would be more likely to have a detrimental effect. You would go to see *Carmen* and take up smoking. You would attend a Goya retrospective and find you suddenly wanted to eat babies. You'd read Dostoyevsky and begin harbouring dark thoughts about the old lady next door. Art does not affect your morals. Art is art and life is life and if you cannot tell the difference, you are to some degree deluded. And I include in that category fundamentalist wowsers of every religious and political hue.

6. *Composers are mysterious and unknowable.*

Well, yes and no (see 5 above). I strongly believe that we all compose, all the time. A surprising amount of our speech is music. It is how we communicate with each other. Only machines speak in a monotone, at an unvaried tempo and without changes of rhythm and dynamic. The meaning behind human speech is in the music as much as the words. More so, in a way. When we speak, the words can say one thing, the music something else. It is because of the musical aspects of speech that we are often able to tell the real meaning behind phrases such as, 'No, of course you're not fat', and, 'I mailed that cheque to you last week, haven't you got it yet?' We tend to be unaware of the rising and falling of our voices as we speak, and we do it without thinking. But similarly, most composers are seldom sure where their own music comes from. To that extent, composing is certainly a mystery, but it is a mystery we all share. And the mystery includes saying what music is about.

7. Symphony concerts are intimidating.

It is often maintained that if only orchestral players were cool and wore jeans, people would flock to concerts. Today's orchestras are determined to seem modern and relevant at all costs. And I do mean all costs: the money spent on image, as opposed to music, would probably astonish most concertgoers. Some orchestras have even hired marketing consultants to tell them that the main problem with their image is the fact that they are called orchestras in the first place. Accordingly, we now have the Melbourne Symphony, the Sydney Symphony and the London Philharmonic. In Western Australia, what was the WASO became the WAS. But how scary can the word 'orchestra' be? Scary to marketing consultants, maybe. Some people seem convinced that audiences will be wooed if only the orchestra — sorry, symphony — gives up wearing evening dress. But really, how intimidating can it possibly be to see ninety or a hundred people on stage dressed in black and white? The rituals associated with orchestral concerts — when to clap, when not to talk — are part of the experience. Even the black and white clothes are there to aid the audience's concentration on the music. And if the listener is able to concentrate, and assuming there is money left after the orchestra's image makeover to pay for adequate rehearsal time, the music is frequently thrilling. The managers of the WAS, incidentally, must have got themselves some new advisers, because not long after they rejected their old name, they re-embraced it. They are the WASO once more. Let's hope all that advice didn't cost too much.

8. Opera is highbrow.

I have always found that going to the opera is a bit like going to the circus, and I am not just thinking of the fat ladies and elephants (which, in the case of the latter, are only in *Aida*, and not always then). It is probably Wagner's fault that opera has the reputation for being intellectually daunting, but remember even *The Ring of the Nibelung* has giants and dwarfs and a big green dragon. Indeed the imagery of *The Ring* — in particular those large-breasted, spear-toting sopranos with plaits and horned helmets — tends to provide the basic tabloid picture of what opera is. But Wagner's operas — which the composer himself called 'music dramas' — are the exception rather than the rule, their extreme length being only one part of the challenge for audiences. Mostly, the continuously evolving musical lines intimidate a lot of listeners because they unfold their argument over many hours, demanding a kind of concentration that is actually rather rare in the opera house (Wagner it was, who first had the idea of dimming the theatre's house lights in order to focus the audience's attention on the stage). Wagner's music is certainly very great, but it is not the be-all and end-all of opera, and the idea that all opera might be 'highbrow' can be held only by people who have had little exposure to the genre. In contrast to Wagner's long lines, the more chopped-up recitative/aria/chorus structure of Mozart's operas and pretty much all Italian opera up to Puccini make rather fewer demands on the listener, because the scenes are comparatively short and the musical character changes every few minutes. Far from requiring a higher degree to appreciate it, much opera benefits from suspension of intellect as well as belief. The plots of comic operas tend towards farce (with a regular admixture of slapstick), while the tragedies are frequently melodramatic tear-jerkers. Of course if you poke around beneath the surface of even the most popular operas — say, those by Donizetti or Verdi — you may begin to discover some of the same complexities that are present in Wagner. But you don't have to do this to have a good time.

9. *Chamber music is more intimidating than orchestral music and more highbrow than opera.*

Unless it is intimidating or highbrow to concentrate, this cliché provides yet more nonsense. Concentration is not as easy for people today as it was before television — in other words, when most chamber music was composed. But the concentration required for chamber music is not necessarily just a matter of time — some chamber pieces are quite short — it is an inward sort of concentration. Remember, before the twentieth century, chamber music was written mostly for performers, not for audiences, and to appreciate chamber music you need to think a bit like a performer. You might try listening to just one of the instruments in a string quartet. Then imagine *being* that instrument, listening to the other three. With a few exceptions, chamber music is classical music at its most conversational, at its most intimate and intense. And the experience of chamber music can be equally intimate and intense.

10. *Classical music is better than other music.*
You do hear this said from time to time. More often, though, it is implied or tacitly believed — even, sometimes, by people who do not listen to classical music at all. They feel they should be listening to it, and that what they are listening to instead is probably not as good. As a result, some of these people become extremely defensive about their own listening habits and will tend to denigrate classical music, often beginning by trotting out clichés 1, 3 and 8. But if classical music is better than other music, what, I wonder, is it better at? It is not better than techno music at keeping people dancing all night long. It is not better than a simple, strophic, modal folk song with countless verses, many repetitions and occasional shifts of melodic emphasis for building the tension in a murder

ballad. As for non-musical uses, Beethoven's *Missa solemnis* is not going to be much good if you're looking for something to listen to while you do the washing-up — at least not if you are hoping to get it over quickly. Western art music is one of the great achievements of our civilisation in the last millennium; there can be no doubt about it. But there is very little point in comparing Rossini with the Rolling Stones, Elgar with Eminem or Stravinsky with the Scissor Sisters because they have so little in common. One type of music is not inherently superior to another any more than beefsteak is superior to bread — and certainly not if your aim is to make toast. Classical music is not better than other sorts of music, but different. In that it comes from a long-standing and continuing tradition of creative endeavour, involving spontaneity and calculation in roughly equal amounts, worked out with the aid of notation and, communicated to its performers in a similar manner, it is unique. Its uniqueness is part of its value. In a real, if tenuous, sense, a composer today is connected via the tradition of notation to composers in the twelfth century. Such connections will become more important, not less, in the present millennium.

An international language?

Music, we are always told, is an international language. The people who insist on this seem very sure they are defining a positive condition. Sometimes, in a distant echo of Gertrude

Stein, we hear that 'music is music', which I suppose amounts to the same thing. Apparently it does not matter where on this planet one travels, music will open those doors that remain stubbornly barred to mere verbal language.

I do not believe that music is an international language. To be precise, I don't believe it is either international or a language. If music were a language, then as the composer Luciano Berio once pointed out, it ought to be possible to say something very precise in it, something like: 'I'm sorry', or ,'Would you please pass the butter?'. It also ought to be possible to translate a spoken language into music and music into a spoken language, doubtless with the same difficulties over semantic nuance encountered in any other translation, but full of confidence, nonetheless, that one's apology will be registered and that one will be handed the butter, not the salt. Nobody seriously believes that this is how music works. With some justification we might describe all or most pieces of music as the products of organisational systems, but certainly not of a single international system.

If music were genuinely international, it would be possible for people in Nagasaki, Nairobi and Noosa equally to appreciate a raga from northern India, mouth music from the Outer Hebrides and Brahms's *German Requiem;* the singing of Kiri Te Kanawa and Tom Waits would both be immediately understood in Sarawak; the intricacies of Chinese opera would be readily comprehended by all sensitive Belgians. I suppose there must be Belgians passionate about Chinese opera, but my hunch is that there are not many of them. And among the citizens of Antwerp and Ghent who do stay home of an evening with their DVDs of *The Peony Pavilion*, there can surely be very few who catch the musical nuances in the same way that an audience in Shaanxi would catch them.

It is possible to find oneself inexplicably moved by all manner of music. I expect that most people have had the experience of being stopped in their tracks by music the like of which they had never before heard. But the key word here is 'inexplicably'. Music — like language — is full of sounds and signs that are culturally specific; even if you understand the words in a foreign language, you will not necessarily catch the subtleties of meaning. For that matter, speaking the same language is itself no guarantee of ready comprehension. I once eavesdropped while someone from Glasgow attempted communication with someone from Birmingham, Alabama. George Bernard Shaw's remark about two countries divided by a common language formed an insistent mental counterpoint to the whole bizarre catastrophe.

Most of those who like to believe that music is an international language know, in fact, that it is nothing of the sort. They are reminded of this every day, because, while wishing music to be pleasant, predictable and reassuring — healing, even — or morally uplifting and inspiring, or at the very least something they can follow and recognise as music, they are always running up against sounds that confound their expectations. Most people can name at least some music that baffles them entirely. Finding themselves in such a situation, some will take offence, going so far as to deny, and vigorously, that what they are listening to is music at all. 'You call that music? *That's* not music.'

There is no reason why a human being should not appreciate all types of music equally, but there is also no very good reason why this should be a common achievement. Most of all, an appreciation of music depends upon experience. If one hears a lot of a particular sort of music, one will very likely come to appreciate it (liking it is another matter). But if one is deprived of opportunities to listen to it in the first place, then obviously there is no reason why one would appreciate it at all. In the context of this wider discussion, Western art music — classical music, the music of the concert hall and the opera house — is a special and urgent case. It is becoming harder and harder to hear this music, and yet I am starting to believe that we need it more and more.

The symptoms of decline

Once classical music was ubiquitous, at least in the Western world. I am thinking not of the eighteenth or nineteenth centuries, but the middle of the twentieth century. I am thinking especially of the heyday of radio, when broadcast concerts of classical music were as common as comedy shows and sports reports. Before television, the whole family tended to listen to the radio as a group. Most homes had just the one radio set and very often the only alternative to listening to it would have been to leave the house. Exposure to classical music, then, was nearly unavoidable. As much as anything, it was through these radio broadcasts that the concept of the 'popular classic' came about, which included works such as Tchaikovsky's Piano Concerto No. 1 in B flat minor and Borodin's 'Polovtsian Dances' from *Prince Igor*, the former still a staple of the repertoire, the latter now on the verge of becoming a rarity in the concert hall (such is the potential fate of anything that is popular or fashionable). In the next room to the radio there was probably a piano, and the chances were there would be someone in the family who could play it reasonably well. There would be a piano stool full of sheet music. This would include some of the hits of the day, but it would also almost certainly feature yet more popular classics: Liszt's *Liebestraum*, say, or Chopin's *Fantaisie-Impromptu* in C sharp minor. There would be songs, too, because if someone in the family played the piano, someone else probably sang. And once again, the average household often failed to distinguish between the songs of Ivor Novello and Schubert. Indeed all the classical pieces I have just mentioned — including the orchestral works — gained extra popularity by having specially composed lyrics put to them, thus themselves becoming pop songs. The big tune from the 'Polovtsian Dances' became 'Stranger in Paradise', and doubtless there are still plenty of older music lovers who find it hard to hear that Chopin impromptu without mentally singing 'I'm Always Chasing Rainbows'.

The gulf that has recently opened between classical music and popular music did not exist in the same way, if at all, just three generations ago. It was in this same era — to be precise the 1930s — that Donald Tovey began to publish widely on music. Tovey's seven volumes of *Essays in Musical Analysis* followed his earlier book *A Companion to Beethoven's Pianoforte Sonatas*. Tovey wrote in plain language and illustrated his texts with dozens of musical examples. Whole chunks taken from the scores of the music under consideration were reproduced to aid the reader's understanding of the analytical points Tovey was making about this Bach fugue or that Beethoven sonata. You are possibly thinking these books sound like textbooks, just the job for a serious student of music. But they were not written for specialists; they were intended for the general public — the *Essays in Musical Analysis* started out as program notes for public concerts — and they were bought by the public in large enough numbers to have remained in print until only a few years ago. A collection of Tovey's writings on chamber music was published as recently as 1989. Tovey's readership was made up of people with broad general educations. They were not only interested enough in classical music to have bought or borrowed the book in the first place, but they were also able to prop it open on the music stand of that piano in their front parlour and make some sense of the examples because access to a piano was common, and piano lessons were a normal part of growing up middle class.

It is almost unthinkable that such books would be published today except by a specialist academic publisher, because classical music in general, and musical literacy in particular, are no longer commonly regarded as core classroom activities. The corollary of this is that classical music has also failed to sustain its place at or near the centre of our cultural life. In fact, it has become marginalised. Today, if you walk into a home with a piano, you find yourself asking who the musician in the house is. And should you want to hear a classical concert on the radio, you will have to tune your receiver to a specialist network.

Not only is classical music considered the property of 'elites' (more of them later) but it has also acquired the capacity to intimidate people. Belief in the cliché that an appreciation of classical music requires a special education puts people on their guard and makes them antagonistic to it. In order to defend classical music against this sort of charge, we need to understand why it is so often levelled, and before we can do that it is essential to ask what it is about classical music that makes it different to other sorts of music. In other words, we must examine precisely those aspects of this music that are not 'international'.

The point of notation

The final two minutes of Gustav Mahler's orchestral song cycle *The Song of the Earth* (*Das Lied von der Erde*) contain some of the most beautiful music I know. I cannot think of anything else in classical music — at least not composed before 1910, when Mahler wrote his piece — that is even similar. The contralto voice repeats, over and over, the German word *Ewig* — 'eternally'. The music is in C major, and at first, the singer's phrases descend cadentially and stepwise from E to D to the keynote C, providing resolution and repose. But then she abandons that final note, her later repetitions taking her only as far as the D. The wished-for eternity now stretches out before us as the vocal line refuses to resolve. It is not only a poignant moment, it is also a famous one.

Oddly enough, the first time I heard this passage I was much more impressed by what was happening behind the singer than I was by the vocal line itself. And to tell the truth it is still the orchestra that I find myself listening to when I hear this piece. The instrumental accompaniment is highlighted by four instruments — a celesta, a mandolin and two harps — which create little splashes of colour on top of a lush bed of sonority from the strings and winds. The sheer sonic allure of this music is ravishing. Even in the context of the rest of the piece, this coda has a special sound: by the time we reach the end of *The Song of the Earth* the music has been playing for about an hour, and yet it is only now, in these last two minutes, that the mandolin appears. The splashes of colour are more than merely decorative; they also bring a sense of weightlessness to the music. They are off the beat, out of time, and gradually they eliminate all sense of pulse. Bit by bit, tempo is vanquished until the music is left floating. This last of the six songs — 'The Farewell' — has no real end. The singer doesn't *want* to say goodbye. The music could go on for ever — eternally — *ewig*. The celesta and the mandolin and the harps play less frequently, less predictably, their once florid figures reduced, bit by bit, to the odd note here and there. The effect is rather like listening to wind chimes agitated by a gentle breeze that gradually drops, then dies; the players might as well be improvising their final desultory contributions. The listener wills the music to continue, but eventually you realise it is no longer there, and a sweet, painful silence ensues.

The delicate balance Mahler achieves in the final moments of *The Song of the Earth* had me curious. It might have sounded a bit like improvisation, but it obviously couldn't have been. So I acquired a copy of the score. As I expected, it quickly became apparent that the music could only have been composed with the help of notation. When you look at the score, it is clear that Mahler has written the music down in such a way as to make sure the four players do not collide with each other. The detail is quite intricate. Those splashes of colour consist of a system of arpeggios of varying speed, outlining the C major chord. The celesta has semiquaver runs up and down a C major arpeggio. One of the harps plays a fragmented, half-speed inversion of this, and the first note of each figure is mostly doubled by the mandolin, the harp then dropping down out of the mandolin's range, creating the rather striking effect of a 'bass mandolin'. The other harp extends this motif, rocking back and forth on a minor third, as if trying to lull the music to its reluctant close. With notation, Mahler has done more than avoid musical collisions; he makes the instrumental patterns intersect and interlock. Far from being improvisation, this is calculation.

It is a paradox. I am suggesting that music which sounds improvised, unstructured, gently disintegrating before our very ears, is actually the result of the kind of careful planning that is only possible when it is worked out on paper. But notation offers more than the possibility of devising intricate musical textures capable of rather precise repetition. There is something about the invention of music on paper (or, these days, often on a computer screen) that distinguishes the very nature of the resulting music from other sorts of music. Notation does not make classical music better or more worthwhile, or even, thanks to a hundred years of sound recordings, longer lasting, but it does make it different. It is that difference that defines the importance of classical music, because it forces it to function in ways that other music cannot.

Patterns, blueprints, maps

All music is also sonic knowledge. No art is created in a social vacuum; inevitably, it is affected by the sights and sounds around us, including other art. Music is composed (or improvised) out of the experience of other music and of life, and at one level it is a form of response to that experience. But there is a problem with this concept. For while most people might accept that literature, and even visual art, can be knowledge, because most novels and a lot of paintings are *about* things, it is more difficult to understand how music performs this role. What is a Bach fugue about?

The difficulty stems from our tendency to associate data with knowledge, and knowledge with meaning. I think it is important to distinguish between these concepts. In classical music, the data are the dots — the notes on the page. That much seems clear. The composer Igor Stravinsky argued that music is incapable of expressing anything but itself, and I find this both an accurate and rather attractive statement, at least as far as it applies to classical music. I might have composed what I consider to be positive, life-affirming music, but you might find it almost unbearably sad (this is not a random example, actually, I often get this response). Music is essentially meaningless — in his 'Barcaldine Suite' the poet Les Murray calls music that 'great nonsense poem' — and insofar as music generates meaning at all, it is surely in the ear of the beholder, varying from listener to listener and from listening to listening.

But knowledge is another matter. Knowledge lies somewhere between data and meaning, being more general than the former but infinitely more specific than the latter. When a group of tribal people share an oral tradition, this is surely knowledge. When a sitar master passes on ragas to a pupil, this is knowledge too. A guitarist joining a rock band needs to acquire the same musical knowledge as the other members in order to fit in. But perhaps the most obvious and widely accepted type of musical knowledge is classical music, because it is also visual data — it is written down, published in books and catalogued in libraries. In other words, it looks like knowledge, and, until quite recently, it was also the only sort of music you could study at a (Western) university.

It is because classical music is written down that there have been, over the centuries, such regular and often radical changes in its style. If you do not record your music, you are forced to remember it, and stylistic fidelity will inevitably be a part of that process of memory: in an oral tradition, you try to pass on a song as accurately as possible or the knowledge is lost. There is also a ritual element to this: in many tribal cultures, it is of great importance that a song is performed the same way every time. One assumes there must be stylistic changes in non-literary musical cultures, if only because human memory and hearing are so fallible (the Chinese whispers effect), but it is virtually impossible to know for certain about shifts of style in oral traditions, precisely because there are no records. Of course, in Western classical music composers have generally tried to notate all facets of their music as accurately as possible. It was because Wagner's music was there in scores to be performed and studied in detail that someone like Debussy could come along a few years later and compose music that was, at one level, heavily influenced by Wagner and, at another level, quite antagonistic to him. This is a form of historical discourse (certainly a form of knowledge) and it is made possible by notation.

All musical knowledge is stored in and makes itself known by the patterns it creates. These are patterns in time as well as space. In classical music, as I have suggested, the patterns are first of all the visual data inscribed by the composer in the score. Some composers imagine complete pieces and then work out the details on the page; others build up a piece from jottings, elaborating them into a larger structure. But it is important to understand that for the classical composer the invention of sound is nearly always partly a visual matter. Because of this, composers since the Middle Ages have been able to construct music that involves the exact repetition of figures or their inversions. Sometimes composers have written musical palindromes, so their pieces sound the same played forwards or backwards. Whether in search of balance or simply as a form of game playing, these are the sorts of patterns that can only be created with the visual aid of notation. Indeed often one cannot identify these patterns by listening to them, one finds them by looking.

Another poet (and novelist), Rodney Hall, wrote: 'We long to fit our minds to someone else's pattern, / To be that person. / So with the pattern of music, / We move in the composer's mind.' In fact, he wrote that in the libretto of a music-theatre piece for which I composed the music. It is called *Whispers*, and it is a kind of mad scene. The central character is an orchestra conductor, and in the piece we watch and listen as he slowly loses his grip on reality while attempting to rehearse Mahler's fourth symphony. Those words, sung by the conductor, describe the hold a musical score — looked at or listened to — can take of a human mind. In the case of this fictional conductor, Mahler's score has taken a rather tenacious and decidedly unhealthy hold. Nevertheless, it is true that for most of us part of the business of being human is the longing 'to fit our minds to someone else's pattern', whether as children listening to stories or as adults falling in love. Music creates abstract patterns that, often enough, allow us to bring our own sense of meaning to bear on what we hear. We surrender to the music, which imposes its patterns on us, but we make of those patterns what we will. The philosopher Mircea Eliade wrote of religious faith turning 'chaos into cosmos'. I think musical patterns have a similar effect on us, at least for the duration of the music.

How do they work? Music — any music, not just classical music — disturbs what passes for silence by creating audible patterns. These are made up of individual sounds of varying colour, intensity and relatedness. Some of the sounds are clearly strung together by the composer, others stand alone waiting to be strung together in the mind of the listener. As we listen, our ears search for connections, for repetition and for change. This process is very similar to the way in which our eyes might scan a painting or a photograph, the major difference being the way in which the work reveals itself to us. You can stand back from a painting and take in the whole image, but it is virtually impossible to do this with a piece of music which gives itself away, second by second, minute by minute, as quickly or as slowly as the composer and performer(s) deem appropriate. We can 'read' a painting from left to right or from right to left, from top to bottom or bottom to top; we can walk right up to the painting and concentrate our attention on a tiny detail. If we read scores, we can do something similar with classical music, but when we listen to performances of those scores we abandon that control. Now we will hear the music in the order the composer wants us to hear it, one thing leading to another. Music in performance is a passing parade.

Now of course that is part of its attraction. Music distorts clock time. Like a drug, it has the capacity to alter our physical states — to raise or lower our pulse — and it is possible for us to lose ourselves in this altered state. But because music is knowledge as well as noise, if we listen carefully we will not lose ourselves; on the contrary, we are more likely to find ourselves. And because musical knowledge is meted out gradually in a time zone of its own making, we not only need to concentrate, we need to remember. We can't stand back, we can't zoom in, we can't reread; all we can do is hang on for the ride and try to remember what has passed before us. The person who wrote the score and the people who work from it — the composer and the performers — may have less need of memory than composers/performers working in an oral tradition, but those who listen to classical music often have a greater need of memory because of the intricacies born of that very notation.

Classical music tends to be loaded with information, and frequently there is an argument of some sort to be followed. If we are listening to a symphony in several movements, particularly if it is on the scale of one by Bruckner or Mahler, we will need to be able to recognise which musical ideas are returning and which we are hearing for the first time. We also need to be able to recognise when familiar ideas are coming back in a modified form and when they are being repeated exactly as before. And, because of memory, even those exact repeats will not seem as they did the first time, since, in the interim, we have heard other music. Described in this way, listening to music seems a surprisingly complicated business. And so it can be, our ears and our memories working in tandem to sift the sonic knowledge and attempt to make some sense of it, perhaps even to bring our own meaning to what we hear, adjusting it as the music continues, gradually forming an overall impression of the entire structure. It is the structure of classical music that is ultimately so important, because that is how this music explains and defines itself. The conductor Adrian Boult used to say that part of his task was to communicate a whole piece, not simply a sequence of episodes. He believed that a symphony resembled a cathedral or some other large building, and he wanted audiences to leave one of his performances as they might leave such a building, taking with them an impression of the entire edifice and what it had felt like to be inside it.

This architectural analogy turns out to be rather versatile. In many ways an orchestral score is similar to a set of architect's drawings, plans for a building that will be constructed in the concert hall before our very ears: the composer is the architect, the orchestra is the team of builders. Unless that concert is recorded, the musical structure built on the night will continue to exist only in the memories of those who were present. Of course, the blueprint or score will remain unchanged (I am ignoring the possibility of corrections and new editions), but each building or performance based upon it — though recognisable in all essentials — will be different from the others in terms of the details of its assembly.

An extreme example of this is the third piano sonata by Pierre Boulez. Composed in 1956 and 1957 but still unfinished, the sonata consists of five movements, only the second and third of which have actually been published. The music of the latter, entitled *Constellation — Miroir*, is presented on large-format pages, so that the player can take in an entire section at a glance. However, the music is not laid out in a conventional linear manner, but rather in discrete clumps, resembling the constellation of the title. If you play this piece, you must find your own way around the constellation. All the music is notated very precisely, but you, the performer, are responsible for the order in which it is presented. Another analogy might be that of a board game: as the pianist finishes a particular passage, there are directions to four more passages. Depending upon which is chosen next, a further four sequences open themselves up. From one performance to the next, the same music might be performed — just as one game of Snakes and Ladders is much the same as another — but the order of events is open-ended and subject to a large number of possible permutations.

As it happens, Boulez's own analogy for this piece is not a blueprint or a board game or, indeed, even a constellation, but the map of a city. The performer is a visitor to this city. The streets and buildings are all marked on the map. Within these fixed parameters, the performer is free to explore.

All classical scores resemble maps to some degree. Mostly they resemble not towns so much as road maps, the resulting performance being a kind of journey. Again, all the streets and landmarks are given, but in a conventional score the route tends to be prescribed. Still, this does not mean there is no freedom for the performer; quite the contrary. A map does not tell you how fast you must travel or by what mode of transport; it does not tell you when you may pause to admire the view. Similarly, a musical score is vague on many issues. Standard musical notation is something of a paradox, being at once quite precise and yet also in some aspects rather open. In most scores, matters of pitch are immutable, and the rhythmic relationships between the pitches leave only the smallest amount of room for manoeuvre. But in other respects a score offers little more than guidelines to a performer. Consider the dynamics of the music, that is to say, how loudly or softly a particular movement or passage or note should be played. A page of a score might be littered with signs instructing the performer to play *forte* and *piano* and *mezzo-forte* and *pianissimo*. But what do these terms really tell us? They are relative terms. They tell us that this note is meant to be louder than that note. But terms such as *forte* and *pianissimo* do not come with decibel readings. My *forte* will probably not be your *forte*. A similar lack of precision applies to matters of tempo. How fast is *allegro*? How slow is *andante*? *Allegro ma non troppo* means 'fast, but not too fast'. But what *is* too fast?

Since Beethoven's time, composers have tried to be more precise about speed, using metronome marks to tell us that the music should move at 126 crotchets to the minute or 52 quavers to the minute or whatever. Not everyone has been persuaded of the efficacy of metronome markings — Wagner, for example, never used them — but it is rare to open a contemporary score and not find fairly precise indications of tempo. But how sacrosanct are these? And what if one ignores them? What if you play, say, the first movement of Beethoven's *Appassionata* sonata very, very slowly, as Glenn Gould did in his infamous 1967 recording? Beethoven did not provide a metronome marking for this piece, but he did carefully inscribe *Allegro assai* at the top of the page, and that means 'rather fast', which is not how Gould played it. And yet, however wilfully odd the tempo of the performance, Beethoven's sonata remains recognisably itself. We are never in danger of mistaking it for another piece, and this would still be true if it were played too quickly or too loudly. On the other hand, if the pitches and rhythms begin to change, then there is a problem. We will move through a stage at which we are hearing the *Appassionata* sonata with a lot of wrong notes, until finally we arrive at an entirely new piece. So I think we can conclude that the pitches and rhythms in this particular piece — the knowledge — are of greater significance than the less-precisely-notated tempo and dynamics. In some twentieth-century music, however, pitch did not have the same vital importance as in Beethoven. Indeed, in the work of composers such as Galina Ustvolskaya and Iannis Xenakis, very often it is a greater sin to play too loudly or too quietly than to play the wrong notes. What characterises all classical scores from all moments in history is an amount of fixed knowledge, some of it more fixed than the rest, all of it subject to the conditions of performance.

Map-reading in the modern world

Because it is written down, classical music has a double life. The pianist Artur Schnabel once said that there is no performance of a Beethoven sonata as great as the work itself. It is, I suppose, a rather obvious point, but it is wholly germane to this present defence. A Beethoven sonata exists for us when we play it or hear it performed, but it also exists silently between the covers, waiting to be opened up and played. Apart from classical music, there is hardly any other music in the world of which this is true. You could not, for example, say that there is no performance of Duke Ellington's 'Sophisticated Lady' as great as the song itself, because there really is no 'song itself': there is no single repository for 'Sophisticated Lady', no place where the real thing exists. An impression of it exists in the memories of singers and jazz instrumentalists and lovers of jazz, but even when it is written down it is an *ex post facto* documentation of a performance or someone's idea of a performance, and it will bear the fingerprints of a particular arranger. Of course, there are also recordings: there is Ella Fitzgerald's 'Sophisticated Lady' and Sarah Vaughan's 'Sophisticated Lady' and Mel Tormé's 'Sophisticated Lady'. These recordings not only have different voices singing the song, they have different combinations of instruments. Moreover, many of the chords and some aspects of the melody are different on each recording. Each performance and recording is unique and, in its way, definitive. But a definitive performance of a Beethoven sonata is impossible. The only definitive Beethoven sonata is the one the composer wrote down.

It follows then that, at one level, classical music is about failure. It is about the greatest pianists in history playing the *Appassionata* sonata (let's keep the same example) and not quite measuring up to the work itself. Because how could you? That is one reason pianists go on playing the piece, and it is one reason that we go on listening to them: not to hear them fail, but to hear them try to make full sense of the score. The score, like a map, will only give us a certain amount of information: a map is not a journey, and a score, in most essentials, does not offer a proper musical experience. Yet, however incomplete the information it contains, a score represents a kind of perfection and, significantly, it is unchanging. There is an important ritual element to musical performance. It is partly a matter of witnessing the unique encounter between the living performer attempting to translate the fixed data of the score into the knowledge of performance. But it is also partly about the (imperfect) repetition of the music. In the same way that many people find comfort and perhaps spiritual enlightenment from hearing the same sentences spoken in church each week, so the repetition of classical music, even when it is very familiar, can create similar feelings in the listener. It is not so much the familiarity that produces this, as the renewal. When a

Christian congregation recites the Lord's Prayer, it is breathing new life into age-old supplications, remaking the prayer in the present — reactivating it, as it were. And when a pianist sets out, yet again, on the *Appassionata* sonata or any other well-known classical piece, something very similar is occurring.

There is a high degree of reliability about classical music. You never finish with the best of it. On the contrary, you establish a partnership with it. You form a relationship, possibly sparked by an initial attraction, later founded on something like love, and you come to know it bit by bit, but never fully. You also know, from the very start, that the music will outlive you. Equally, again as in human relationships, sometimes you never really get started with a piece; you simply fail to hit it off, or you get off to a flying start but the next morning realise you've made a terrible mistake — you can't begin to think what you ever heard in the piece. With the good experiences, as with all worthwhile relationships, you need to work on them. An appreciation of classical music grows the more you listen, the more attention you pay, the more you *try*; most pieces do not give themselves up to instant comprehension. That is to say — and again, it is like relationships — after that initial attraction across a crowded concert hall, the appreciation of a classical piece needs time and effort before it will have very much meaning.

I think this is the cause of some of those classical music clichés. As far as the mass media are concerned, all this time and effort make classical music rather unfashionable. The media are mostly concerned with what *is* fashionable; they are concerned with novelty and, by definition, novelty does not last. The idea that a piece of music might require time to appreciate, that it cannot be summed up instantly in 400 words, is anathema to most media proprietors and not a few arts editors, and so classical music is relegated to a minor place in the arts pages. Fewer classical concerts and recordings are reviewed; music that, within living memory, was at the centre of Western civilisation has been re-branded, by people who know nothing about it, as a recherché indulgence for 'elites'. When classical music is discussed, at least in the English-language print and electronic media, there is a common tendency to have the discussion at the most fundamental level possible. Presumably this is an attempt to demystify highbrow art for the average reader, and so it must always be assumed that the reader knows absolutely nothing. Everything, then, is addressed to beginners, since we do not want to put people off with technical jargon.

This is frankly odd, because it does not obtain in most other areas of the media. Take economics. I freely admit to knowing very little about this subject. For example, I do not really know what the Australian All Ordinaries index is or how it works. I do not understand why the price of a barrel of West Texas crude should be significant. And yet not a day goes by but I am subjected to reports on the stock market that employ jargon of this sort. Clearly we are all now meant to be interested in economics; that is what the media tell us. We are also expected to understand the technical jargon involved in sport — you don't hear cricket commentators explaining the leg-before-wicket rule every time it is mentioned. Television weather forecasters assume we all know what hectopascals are. But the same media that would have us be experts in economics, sport and weather systems also tell us that classical music is for specialists. Where once the daily newspaper could be relied upon as a source of critical debate regarding classical concerts and operas — and this was often quite helpful in developing a love and understanding of the music in the reader — today there are far fewer column inches devoted to reviews.

It is not just newspapers that have changed. Only a generation ago, politicians thought culture was a good thing. Perhaps significantly, over the past two or three decades there has been a change in the meaning of the word 'culture' itself. Now it most often turns up directly after the adjective 'popular'. The other context in which it is sometimes used is basically derogatory: I am thinking of expressions such as Robert Hughes's 'the culture of complaint'. And there is also what socially conservative politicians in Australia, believing that public broadcasting is thwarting their plans for a new world order, like to call 'the culture of the ABC'. But culture once meant art — I suppose these days we are forced to call it *high* art — and conservative politicians in particular believed in it because it was thought to represent the pinnacle of Western civilisation. It was, in fact, a significant part of what those conservatives were trying to conserve. Small-l liberals, on the other hand, believed you did not merely conserve culture, you had to subsidise it; you brought it to the masses via public education, public libraries and public broadcasting. And, note, they wanted to bring culture to people. They were not talking about making art accessible; on the contrary, the idea was to make people accessible to art.

So what has happened here? Why do politicians no longer seem to believe in literature and public libraries, in paintings and art galleries, in classical music and publicly funded orchestras? I think the answer is obvious. Put simply, most modern politicians are rather disappointing people. Like those who run the mass media, today's Western politicians care mostly about economics. They have also bought all of those classical music clichés, so that providing vigorous support for orchestras or opera companies would, they believe, be political suicide. It would mean lining up with all those despised elites.

It is worth dwelling for a moment on this word. Politicians have been dumping on the elites for a long time, but I am still trying to discover who they are. Obviously when politicians talk about elites they don't mean very rich people, because that would include quite a few of them. It must be some other sort of elite, then. Do they mean people who are well educated? There would certainly be fewer of them in modern politics. But I thought it was generally accepted that the country needed well-educated people, so it probably isn't them either. Is it, then, people who are simply the best at what they do? Clearly not, for this would include sporting figures and they are beyond reproach. Perhaps it is people with imaginations the politicians so disapprove of. That would certainly rule out nearly all of their own number. In the end, though, I suspect the people we are talking about are people who think for themselves and ask difficult questions. They have always been unpopular with politicians, and in the age of spin they are a genuine threat to the way modern governments like to conduct business. But the point is that, whoever these elites are, they are very bad people, just a notch above asylum seekers.

Linked to the long-running doublespeak about elites is another piece of pure nonsense that I enjoy for its twisted logic. It goes like this: the arts — and here classical music is a prime example — are patronised by the elites; why, therefore, should ordinary people — 'mums and dads' — subsidise them? (Note that although when politicians refer to elites they are probably not speaking of wealthy people, in the fully constructed public myth the elites always have money to burn, especially on the arts.) This is the user-pays argument and, depending upon whether you believe it or not, it is self-fulfilling or self-defeating. We should not subsidise the arts because they are for the elites who can well afford to pay; but if we do not subsidise the arts, they will always be only for the elites who can afford to pay. Modern Western governments like to save money. The arts are an easy target so long as the majority of voters can be persuaded that things such as classical music are only for the kind of people they don't really like.

The consolation of the musical map

We will wait a long time before politicians of genuine vision come along. We will wait even longer before we have politicians whose word we can trust. The spinning may never be done. And yet it is modern politicians, so drab and dispiriting, so uninspiring in the roles for which they were elected, that, in part at least, have recently inspired in me a new appreciation of classical music and have helped me to see, perhaps for the first time in my life, just what that music is for.

Over the last decade or so, as my disillusionment has grown with the way the modern world is being run, I have to some extent found myself taking refuge in classical music. I have always listened to music a lot — a lot more, I'm well aware, than many other composers — and my listening is very broad. Jazz is a particular passion, and in particular I listen to a lot of modern jazz. I have given up trying to stay fully abreast of rock music, but in addition to classic rock from the last forty years, and not forgetting figures such as Dylan and Van Morrison who continue to produce new music, my CD collection contains albums by the likes of Radiohead and Eminem. I like country music, especially the classics. Few things move me more than the blues. I have liked Anglo-Celtic folk music since childhood and today I like it more than ever. And so on. My tastes, you see, are catholic. So I find it significant that more and more I am drawn to classical music. A quarter of a century after my formal music education, which was exclusively classical, came to an end, I not only listen to more Bach and Beethoven and Mahler than ever, I even buy scores of their music. The more the world of public affairs repels me, the more I am drawn to Haydn and Mozart. You will say, perhaps, that this is escapism, but I don't think it is.

On the one hand, we have politicians lying to us, being publicly exposed as liars and then attempting to spin their way out of trouble. The most common technique, it seems, is to deny everything. In the face of compelling evidence, they get up in their parliament or on our TV screens and say that they did not lie because they 'honestly believed' they were telling the truth. Anyway, they cannot now quite remember what they were told. And, thinking back, they had a bad mobile connection on the morning they were passed the advice, so they probably misheard. Or perhaps they were given the wrong advice. Or, more likely still, nobody told them anything at all. About anything. Ever. After all, they are only the prime minister and his cabinet, why would they be kept informed? On and on it goes, day after day, week after week, until the public is so sick of the lying that we just want it to stop. We want to forget about it — which is precisely what the politicians hope will happen. It's called toughing it out.

And then, on the other hand, there is Brahms. This is not escapism; it is a form of consolation. A retreat certainly, but a retreat, I would argue, *into* reality rather than away from it. There is no spin in Brahms.

In September 2001, when the aeroplanes hit the World Trade Center towers and the Pentagon, we were quickly told that the world had changed forever. In a way I suppose it did. There have always been terrorists, just as there have always been lying politicians, but the scale of September 11 was new, and so was the real-time TV coverage of the atrocity. Like most people, I suppose, I was in shock for a while. One thing I certainly didn't want was music. For a few days, even the greatest music seemed trivial. But, shortly after, I found I had a bigger appetite for it than ever. It was classical music I wanted, and in particular the string quartets of Brahms.

Brahms has always been a favourite of mine and the more I have listened, the more I have come to admire his music. Even in the composer's lifetime, his pieces were never very fashionable. He was a conservative figure who eschewed flamboyance. Perhaps that was a small part of the attraction for me. When, in the days after September 11, I began to want to hear music again, the first thing I seemed to need was the sound of the string quartet. Part of this was probably the sonic balm that Brahms's string writing creates, that burnished mellowness that no other composer has ever quite matched. Bartók, for example, would have been quite the wrong composer for those particular weeks. But there was also the symbolism inherent in the sound of the string quartet, of the four players blending with each other and yet retaining their independence. On a rather simplistic level, I suppose, the string quartet offers a musical analogy of cooperation and democracy, and that in itself was appealing.

Then there was the matter of duration. It was important that the music I heard lasted long enough for me to, as it were, enter its world. I needed to sit still for a period and concentrate: I suppose I needed to meditate. But I also needed the music to last long enough to allow me to climb inside these string quartets — not to lose myself, but to explore the musical ideas and arguments. That was another important aspect of the music, that ideas were stated — beautifully, eloquently — and then tossed around by the composer, developed, thought through, talked over, analysed in real time. This was very much in contrast to a lot of the rubbishy rhetoric that came through the media from politicians and pundits on all sides after September 11. Bellicose or gloating, scary or sanctimonious, it was nearly all revolting to hear. The Brahms quartets, though, offered those abstract patterns — perfectly reasonable, and with no words at all.

Finally, I needed the string quartets of Brahms at that point in history and at that point in my life because for more than a century they had been performed and listened to and studied, thought about by players and audiences and musicologists. One of the great joys of classical music (and I guess this goes for all great art of a certain age) is that you can discover works for the first time, knowing, in a sense, that you can trust them because they have been valued by earlier generations. Up until this moment, you see, I did not know the Brahms string quartets. I already knew and loved the quintets and the sextets. And ever since my teenage years I had known the piano quintet and the clarinet quintet. It seemed likely that the string quartets, which had evaded my attention for forty-four years, would not disappoint me. Even if they turned out not to be among the composer's greatest masterpieces — and I think it's true to say they are not — I knew they would give me what I needed. They would provide me with reassurance, they would bring me the consolation I sought.

I use the word 'consolation' very deliberately. The Brahms string quartets made me feel there was goodness in the world. The essentially pointless business of creativity made me feel there was a point to life. The fact that the quartets were composed at all, back in the nineteenth century; the fact that they have been played and listened to with attention ever since; the fact that they are still played and listened to: it was all consoling.

In 1936, the German conductor Wilhelm Furtwängler wrote in his notebook that art 'in the usual sense' provides 'an expression of life', but 'great art' is an 'orientation' of life. You can be sure that Furtwängler was thinking of classical music, particularly music in the Austro-German tradition, and I find it interesting to run up against another version of that map analogy. When Furtwängler writes of 'great art' as an 'orientation', however, he is taking the analogy a stage further. This is more than spotting similarities between a score and a map: Furtwängler is claiming that music provides orientation in our lives and of our lives. It provides our lives with focus and perspective and direction. Brahms's music certainly did that for me in 2001.

The composer

There is a poem by W. H. Auden called 'The Composer'. In it, Auden compares Brahms's job to that of other artists. It begins: 'All the others translate ...' He is alluding to the impossibility of music having any concrete meaning outside its own frame of reference. It is similar to Stravinsky's maxim about music being powerless to express anything but itself: music is Les Murray's 'great nonsense poem', Rodney Hall's 'pattern'. Auden goes on: '... only your notes are pure contraption'. In other words, music — pure music — is not *about* anything, it *is* something. There's nothing to interpret — nothing to 'translate' — music is the thing itself. Again I find that reassuring, consoling.

This probably sounds naïve. I seem to be suggesting that Brahms can cure the ills of the modern world. I wish he could. I wish his music could convince terrorists of the wrongness of what they do. I wish it could function as a truth drug for politicians. Of course that is not what I am claiming. But I am claiming that music has a vital role to play if we are to keep going. When we listen to music, we plug ourselves into something positive. I am not sure you can compose a negative string quartet. Auden's poem says that only music is 'unable to say an existence is wrong'. We have heard a lot of that in the first years of the twenty-first century. There have been a lot of people — mostly politicians and terrorists — saying that other people should not exist.

Classical music reaffirms creativity because it has survived. It connects us to the best of civilisation at a time when we find little that is civilised in our own world. This sounds vaguely nostalgic, I know, but nostalgia is not the attraction of classical music any more than it is the attraction of Shakespeare. When we listen to Brahms or Wagner or Mahler or Mozart, we are directly connected to a creative mind — *directly* ('All the others translate ... only your notes are pure contraption') — and we are able, for as long as the music lasts, to 'fit our minds to someone else's pattern'. That is why classical music has survived and why people still need it. That is also why those of us who love classical music need to fight for it. We need to dispel the suggestion that classical music is for elites — whoever they are. It is for anyone who will take the time to listen. It is not 'difficult'; it is just that it will not give up all its secrets in one go. And it will never surrender itself to market forces, however much the market might want it to. Very often when we read about classical music today, it is some gloomy story about the bottom dropping out of the recording industry. Apparently nobody buys classical CDs any more. This is not, in fact, true. It is just that CDs are not selling in the kind of numbers the big record companies would like. It is an economic crisis, not a musical one, but to hear the executives of some of the major record companies talk, you would think it was Mozart's fault their profits are down. The truth is that after those executives and their companies have gone to the wall, Mozart will still be around, reliable as ever.

For most of 2001, I was composing a long song cycle called *Learning to Howl*. It was a setting of poems from across the ages, mostly by women. After September 11, I stopped for a time. Just as I didn't want to listen to music, I also didn't want to compose it. Even when I felt like composing again, it seemed to me that setting to music little poems by Emily Dickinson and Sappho and Christina Rossetti was perhaps no longer the most relevant activity. Like a lot of artists, I imagine, I cast around for something to say about what had happened in New York and Washington and what I feared might happen next. I wanted to say something profound. I wanted to say something helpful, something useful. Nothing came. And then it struck me that the most useful thing I could do — and perhaps even the most profound — was to continue as before; to go on imagining sounds, jotting them down, moving them around on the page, trying to get them to come out right so as to add to the body of musical knowledge. It seemed to me that we needed more patterns, more maps than ever. Our lives needed more orientation. Part of this realisation was also to do with a tradition that had gone on for centuries. Brahms's music had sustained me; now, it seemed, I had almost a duty to add to that tradition, however poor my addition might seem besides the great works of the past. We need the tradition now more than ever, and so we need to protect it. The only way to protect a tradition is to continue it.

That is one reason I find those closing moments of *The Song of the Earth* so moving and so important. It is the sound of a composer not wanting to let go (Mahler was ill, and in fact was dead by the time the piece was performed). It is the sound of a piece not wanting to end ('ewig, ewig'). It is the sound of a tradition of artistic endeavour that will continue to sustain us, even when the rest of our world so badly lets us down.

Auden's poem ends like this:

You alone, alone, imaginary song,
Are unable to say an existence is wrong,
And pour out your forgiveness like a wine.

PART TWO

Ten Composers

The tears of
John Dowland

Music to hear, why hear'st thou music sadly?

Sweets with sweets war not, joy delights in joy:

Why lov'st thou that which thou receiv'st not gladly,

Or else receiv'st with pleasure thine annoy?

If the true concord of well-tunèd sounds,

By unions married, do offend thine ear,

They do but sweetly chide thee, who confounds

In singleness the parts that thou shouldst bear;

Mark how one string, sweet husband to another,

Strikes each in each by mutual ordering,

Resembling sire and child and happy mother,

Who, all in one, one pleasing note do sing;

Whose speechless song, being many, seeming one,

Sings this to thee: 'Thou single wilt prove none'.

Shakespeare's Sonnet VIII is addressed to someone who, in modern parlance, is scared of commitment. He — it almost certainly is a young man — is reproached by the poet for failing to appreciate the benefits that come from being part of a family: bachelorhood is all very well, but it will lead nowhere; to be a family man, that's the thing.

I have always liked the poem for its musical analogy. It is, of course, overextended, but I expect Shakespeare knew that. I also think he must have known that the entire conceit was pretty arch. He expresses surprise that the person to whom the sonnet is addressed should hear music sadly. But isn't that how all cultured Elizabethans and Jacobeans listened to music? Surely Shakespeare is intending a joke here; he is mocking the melancholy soul who would sigh and weep in the presence of beauty, just as, in *As You Like It*, he sweetly chides the gloomy Jaques. Another melancholic from the plays is Jessica in *The Merchant of Venice*, who tells Lorenzo in the final act, 'I am never merry when I hear sweet music'.

I have to say I feel some empathy for Jessica. Like her, and like the man in the sonnet, I also hear music sadly, or at least quietly, and, if possible, with a fair bit of concentration. After listening to music, I am often alone in my thoughts; melancholy, you might say. It is occasionally remarked on by my friends, moreover, that, while I'm known in general to be possessed of a cheerful disposition, the music I compose is anything but cheerful. I've heard words such as 'sad', 'passionate' and 'disguising pain' used as descriptions of some of my pieces. And I can see what people mean. But the thing is, I never set out deliberately to compose 'sad' music. It just seems to happen.

There are two related concepts running in parallel here. First there is 'sweet' music — the 'true concord of well-tunèd sounds' — that is pleasant to hear, and yet received 'not gladly'. And then there is 'sad' music, whatever that is. To a degree, sadness or happiness in music is surely a matter for the listener. When you stop to think about it, naming a great piece of music that is entirely 'happy' is no easy feat. Mendelssohn's *Italian* symphony, perhaps? The same composer's Octet? Could Beethoven's Symphony No. 8 be a contender? And why should we think of this music as happy anyway? Is it simply to do with major keys, swift tempos and dance-like rhythms? The response created in me by such music is far more likely to be physical than mental — the sound of it quickens my pulse. Perhaps happy feelings are somehow related to that. But as a rule, I think, most music is better at making us sad — at any rate reflective — than it is at making us happy. And it is particularly bad at telling jokes: just think of all those heavy-handed attempts by Mozart.

So why do we listen to music, if it is likely to depress us? Well I don't believe that music, even sad music, does make us depressed. Rather the opposite. After all, plenty of people choose to watch sad movies specifically in order to have a good cry, and they seem to emerge from the experience somehow purged. By the same token, people will deliberately attend horror films in order to have their wits scared out of them. Both sorts of film induce temporary states — of sadness or of fear — that, in part at least, serve to put the viewer's own life in perspective. Perhaps these experiences even make us feel better about ourselves. They provide us with a swift, if often artificial, catharsis. But it is also true that, as the final credits roll, we feel we have endured, just as the hero or heroine of the film has endured; we have emerged stronger, perhaps nobler. This attitude certainly chimes with the attitude to melancholy that Shakespeare was mocking in his sonnet.

Like most Elizabethan fashions — and melancholy was as much a fashion as a malady — this one came from continental Europe. The Renaissance physic recognised four humours: sanguinity, choler, phlegm and melancholy. Ideally these would balance each other in perfect proportion. But since human beings have seldom been perfectly balanced, even in the Renaissance when man was held to be 'the measure of all things', one humour always tended to dominate. Accordingly, people were sanguine (good humoured) or choleric (prone to angry rages) or phlegmatic (lacking in passion) or melancholic (subject to inexplicable bouts of sadness or fear). Of the four, you might think melancholy would be the least desirable.

But this was true only to a point. In Albrecht Dürer's engraving *Melencolia I* (1514), a winged figure sits slumped and disconsolate. At his feet lie abandoned carpenter's tools — a plane, a chisel, a set square, some nails. On the wall behind him is a calendar and beside it an hourglass, the lower part of which is nearly full of sand. Nothing is happening and time is running out. Anyone who has ever lived through a home renovation will recognise the scene. But the melancholy figure with his chin resting on his hand is not merely dejected. There is also something noble about him. This is, after all, the same pose adopted by Rodin's 'Thinker'. When we consider the fellow in the engraving we are looking at a representation of civilisation. Dürer's winged man might be sad, but he is also sensitive, indeed angelic. As Aristotle pointed out, all good philosophers and artists share a melancholy temperament. So is this a melancholy artist we are looking at?

The Elizabethans regarded the melancholy state with a degree of ambivalence. If not perhaps something devoutly to be wished for oneself, it was at least to be admired in others. And if you did happen to suffer from it, you could be proud of the fact, not least because of the Aristotelian association of melancholy with philosophical and artistic endeavour. The Elizabethan composer Anthony Holborne composed a number of pieces inspired by and essentially celebrating melancholy: 'The Sighes', 'The Image of Melancholly', 'The Teares of the Muses' and 'The Funerals' are some of his titles. The tempo is always slow and so is the rate of harmonic change; the melodic lines droop and fall. It is music that encourages stillness and seriousness in the listener. The titles speak of creative endeavour and death. Art is a way of putting off death, but it is also a way of coming to terms with it. Holborne's art, which stares death in the face, might be the musical equivalent of a *memento mori*, but then at some level all music has this function. That in itself might explain the melancholy demeanour of Shakespeare's young man.

Holborne died in 1602, just a year before Elizabeth I. The sombre national mood that followed the Queen's death made Jacobean England an even more melancholy place than Elizabethan England had been, ripe for literary dissection in Robert Burton's vast tract *The Anatomy of Melancholy* (1621).

One of the day's most famous composers — an almost exact contemporary of Shakespeare, and so, like the playwright, straddling the Elizabethan and Jacobean eras — was also a famous melancholic. John Dowland summed up the condition in both songs and consort music. His signature piece, a pun on his own name (which he pronounced 'Doeland'), was entitled *Semper Dowland semper dolens* ('Always Dowland, always gloomy').

Some of Dowland's songs make it clear that a woman is responsible for this state of mind. As with the late-mediaeval troubadours, Elizabethan and Jacobean love songs often tell of a hapless suitor treated with cruel indifference, and consequently wallowing in self-pity. But more typically, Dowland's songs describe a general melancholy. We may attribute this to his own circumstances. Continually refused favour at Elizabeth's court, he was forced to abandon his homeland and work for the King of Denmark. Dowland often returned to the theme of exile in his songs. In 'Sorrow Stay', composed at Elsinore and published in his *Second Booke of Songs or Ayres* (1600), the poet views his melancholy condition as an emotional and spiritual purgative, pleading with 'sorrow' itself to 'lend true repentant tears / To a woeful wretched wight'. In 'Flow My Tears', which is perhaps Dowland's single most famous song, the singer bemoans his exile: 'Where night's black bird her sad infamy sings / There let me live forlorn.' Again there is a strong suggestion of wallowing in his sadness, and more than a touch of self-dramatising: 'Happy, happy they that in hell / Feel not the world's despite!'

'Flow My Tears' was one of the most famous tunes of Dowland's day. Originally a purely instrumental pavan entitled simply *Lachrimae* (Tears), it became, in 1604, the foundation of a book of consort music, *Lachrimae or Seaven Teares*. Dowland dedicated it to Anne of Denmark, the Danish king's sister, and, as it happened, the wife of James I, Elizabeth's successor, writing in his preface that 'no doubt pleasant are the tears which Musicke weeps, neither are tears shed always in sorrow, but some time in joy and gladness'.

The original *Lachrimae* melody is treated to a series of variations in the book, with the opening motif always prominent. This figure is characterised by four descending notes that, in a stock gesture of Renaissance musical word-painting, represent those flowing tears. But tears or not, the melodic contour is familiar enough. It is what the German ethnomusicologist Curt Sachs liked to call a 'tumbling strain'. According to Sachs, in 'primitive' musics such as Native American chant, the voice of the singer begins on a high note and then the pitch tumbles down to the end of the phrase. We may no longer care much for the word 'primitive', but Sachs's theory still holds plenty of water. Most traditional

Aboriginal singing has just the same contours. It is hardly surprising. This is the manner of speech, in particular of public speech, and since most songs are a heightened form of public speech, it seems rather obvious that the most 'natural' sort of melodic contour will be a 'tumbling strain'. It could be because I am 400 years too late, but in Dowland's *Lachrimae* I don't hear musical tears at all. I hear the reassurance of a human voice. And this is true even when the music is played by a solo lute or a consort of viols.

Is it such reassurance that we listen for in music? Is this, perhaps, what makes us contemplative, melancholy even, when we listen to certain pieces? And if so, what kind of piece might have this effect on us? Tempo is surely important. So, I would think, is the music's prevailing gentleness. Perhaps in order to be contemplative a piece of music ought not have too much harmonic movement. I am reminded of the so-called 'swoon' phenomenon. 'Swoon' was a regular segment on ABC Classic FM when Christopher Lawrence presented the early morning program in the 1990s. Lawrence always insisted that there was no formula behind what he called his 'tiny parcels of rapture'; the pieces on the best-selling CD compilations were there, as often as not, in response to listener demand, always a good way to bring about a best-seller. But if there was not a formula, there was certainly a pattern. There were no fast 'swoon' pieces, no loud ones and no 'dissonant' ones. Lawrence's daily five-minute musical oasis attracted its share of criticism — though the critics were easily outnumbered by the fans — and it is true there was a fast-food quality to the home-delivered rapture, but it still seems to me that this segment of his program encouraged, if only for five minutes after the eight o'clock news, the idea of being still with the music; listening to music, rather than simply overhearing it.

The figure in Dürer's *Melencolia I* might be listening to music, hearing it 'sadly' like the young man in Shakespeare's sonnet. Perhaps he is enjoying the catharsis of tears. Perhaps these are even, as Dowland suggests, tears of happiness. There again, perhaps he is contemplating the power of the human voice, even when represented by an instrument, to offer solace and balm. And perhaps, like Anthony Holborne, he is staring at death..

In 1976, the English composer Harrison Birtwistle composed a work inspired by Dürer's engraving. Birtwistle's *Melencolia I* is scored for solo clarinet, harp and two string orchestras, and the piece is in one big slow movement lasting about half an hour. It is a particularly intense experience, the complex musical argument laid out in relentless slow motion, the predominantly quiet surface of the music just about managing to conceal a pent-up violence that finally breaks through in a shocking, screaming outburst from the clarinet. There's not much balm here, not by the end.

An audience really must want to listen to this piece, or at the very least be in a receptive frame of mind. This is no five-minute 'swoon'. Come to think of it, Birtwistle's *Melencolia I* asks for the kind of concentration depicted in Dürer's *Melencolia I*. The audience must make an effort.

I once discussed this issue with the composer. Birtwistle's response was to shrug. 'One can very easily get into this terrible Hollywood, hour-and-a-half syndrome, where you have to have something happening every five minutes,' he said. 'And that's not what my music's about. I can't reduce everything to the expectancy of people's concentration. I'm not responsible for people's concentration problems. A piece must be the right length.'

Music offers the listener all manner of experiences. It can stimulate as well as soothe; in addition to solace and balm, it can bring challenge and agitation. Birtwistle's *Melencolia I*, indeed, brings all of these in different measure. But whatever the nature of the music, the act of intense listening, even in an auditorium with 2000 other people, is necessarily a solitary, even lonely, act. As Birtwistle says, the audience is responsible for its concentration problems. Overcoming those problems, entering the music, listening hard: this will often be a melancholy experience, and not least because, as Holborne, Dowland and Shakespeare knew, it will remind us of our own humanity, and therefore of our mortality.

Music to order by Franz Joseph Haydn

The idea that great music may be composed to order sits uneasily in the modern public consciousness. Most people like to believe that a symphony is inspired by some higher power — higher than a commissioning body, that is — and that the notes cannot just be summoned at will. Popular culture presents high art as the product of tormented souls, of artists struggling with their personal demons, usually culminating in one of those sudden flashes of Inspiration when the Art comes pouring out. We've all seen it in films.

But you cannot write the sheer quantity of music that Bach, Haydn and Mozart did with inspiration alone. This level of creative output does not happen if you sit around waiting to feel inspired. True inspiration, as the artist Eugène Delacroix observed, is being at your desk by nine in the

1. Attendance at the event is deemed to be acceptance of these terms and conditions which could be during a suitable break – interval is scheduled for the applicable performance and this ticket is subject to any conditions for that activity and/or performance.

2. Venue access and the route for guided tours are subject to venue availability and rehearsal schedules. Ticket holders must remain with the tour group at all times and follow instructions. There are 200 to 300 stairs on a tour and rubber soled shoes should be worn.

3. Advertised programs or tours may be varied without notice. Artists may be added, withdrawn or substituted for performances and the right to vary prices, venues, seating arrangements and audience capacity is reserved.

4. Venue access and the route for guided tours be used inside Sydney Opera House, unless expressly authorised. Sydney Opera House reserves the right to broadcast or telecast any event. No food or drink is allowed inside a venue unless specified.

5. Ticket holders enter the venue at their own risk. Sydney Opera House will not be responsible for any loss, damage or injury arising out of the use of, attendance at or the use of any of these conditions.

6. Any bag or item larger than A4 must be cloaked and may be inspected.

7. Camera, video and audio recorders may not

This ticket may not, without the prior written consent of Sydney Opera House be resold for commercial packages or at a premium, nor may it be packaged or used for advertising, promotional or other commercial purposes. If a ticket is sold in breach of this condition, the bearer of the ticket may be refused admission.

The right of admission is reserved by the management. Latecomers will not be able to join a tour and will only be admitted to a

SYDNEY OPERA HOUSE

SYDNEY OPERA HOUSE CONCERT HALL   Door 7

UMCMP, ANDREW MCMANUS
AND LIMELIGHT PRESENT

CECILIA BARTOLI

Sun 13 March 2011   8:00 PM

$255.00   Box A22

CONCERT HALL
13 Mar 11
ORDER: 24512440
TKT: 8083181

Reedemable for 1
copy of
Cecilia Bartoli's
new album
Sospiri

Prem+CD
$255.00

morning. It is also recognising when you have come up with something that really works. Artists are researchers, inventors, continually trying things out. Like scientific researchers, composers have hunches and they perform experiments — in their heads, on paper, at the workbench of the piano or in the laboratory of the rehearsal room. It is time-consuming, this research, and composers must eat, so somehow the work has to be funded. In the second half of the twentieth century the job of funding artistic experimentation often fell to governments, either directly or, as with a lot of scientific research, through universities. One cannot generalise about the nature of the music that resulted from music's time on the campus, although I think it is fair to point out that academic life thrives on original thinking, in particular the kind that can be written up in a report and published and which often tends to be theoretical. But the composers of the classical era, of Haydn's time, were never likely to be awarded government grants. The great patron of music in eighteenth-century Europe was the aristocracy, and it was a rare prince indeed who demanded experimentation. Mostly, princes like to be amused.

Franz Joseph Haydn (1732–1809) spent thirty years serving the Esterházy family, first Prince Paul, then his son Nikolaus. He lived at the family's palace at Eisenstadt, south of Vienna, and then later at the new Esterháza Castle across the border in Hungary, and he was a member of the household staff. Even after his promotion to chief Kapellmeister he was really only a rung or two above the

Esterházys' cook. His responsibilities included care of the in-house orchestra, both its players and its instruments, and the production of music for concerts and dinners, as well as religious services and operas. The majority of Haydn's symphonies were composed during this time, and by the end of his life there were a lot of them, 104 with official numbers and three or four others. With the Esterházys' permission, Haydn was also allowed to accept outside jobs, and mostly these consisted of smaller works such as string quartets, but as his fame grew outside central Europe, partly courtesy of pirated publications filled with inaccuracies, he began to receive offers of grander commissions. The six so-called 'Paris' symphonies, for example, were composed during the mid-1780s at the request of the Comte d'Ogny, and they were conceived on a scale befitting the very large orchestra of Le Concert de la Loge Olympique, a group of Parisian Freemasons that included the Comte himself. Haydn's last symphonies were all composed in the early 1790s for the London-based violinist and impresario, J. P. Salomon. The success of six of these in his Hanover Square concerts was so great that Salomon commissioned a further set for concerts at the King's Theatre in the Haymarket, so there are twelve 'London' symphonies in all, numbered 93 to 104 in Haydn's bulging catalogue. By this time, Prince Nikolaus had died, and although still technically on the staff of Nikolaus's unmusical son, Prince Anton, Haydn was now free to live wherever he liked, to travel and freely to accept commissions such as those from Salomon. However, the composer's last years were spent back with the Esterházys, this time working for Nikolaus's grandson on a part-time basis, and it was this final decade of Haydn's life — the first decade of the nineteenth century — that saw the composition of *The Creation*, *The Seasons* and the last six great masses.

So Haydn was anything but the nineteenth-century Romantics' idea of an artist, heroically asserting his independence and flying in the face of the status quo. He was a servant, later an artisan. And yet of course he was also one of the very greatest innovators in musical history. He might not have invented the keyboard sonata, the string quartet or the symphony, but he developed each genre and brought it to maturity. From a formal point of view, Haydn's influence is heard not only in the work of the composers who immediately followed him — Beethoven, Schubert, Mendelssohn, Schumann — but also among the later Romantics, such as Bruckner and Mahler, on into the twentieth century and even our own time. How did he achieve such distinction, given that all his life he was working to order?

Haydn's own theory about this was that the comparative isolation he experienced in the Esterházys' frankly provincial palaces forced him to be original. It seems a particularly diplomatic theory, the sort of theory you might hit upon if you were asked the question with your employer in the room. Would it not, for one thing, be equally plausible to assume that being cut off from the main cultural centres might result in creative stagnation?

In fact Haydn seems to have thrived on the workload he was given and on the specific demands of his employers. Prince Nikolaus, for example, was a devout man, and one of the most striking innovations of Haydn's early symphonies is the way in which they often include liturgical references, particularly in the form of plainsong. This was much more significant than it might sound to us. Today we are used to composers who quote other music. It's a postmodern commonplace. But Haydn wasn't just quoting. The symphony, in the form he inherited it from such minor composers as Sammartini, Wagenseil and the brothers Graun, was little more than an undifferentiated piece of orchestral music and generally rather high-spirited. Opera overtures were known as symphonies ('sinfonias'). The interludes in an oratorio were called symphonies. There is a minute-long 'pastoral symphony' in Handel's *Messiah* which is really just a peasant dance to get us in the mood for the arrival of the shepherds. The word certainly did not carry the overtones of high seriousness and structural complexity that it has today. Haydn was the first composer to bring seriousness to his symphonies and the first to make them complex — not always, but often enough — and it happened while he was in the employ of the Esterházys. One of the ways he did this was by using plainsong themes. For example, the so-called 'Lamentatione' symphony (No. 26), composed around 1768, used Gregorian chants associated with Easter. It was also in a minor key throughout. This was no longer music as entertainment, it was music to be meditated upon, and it came about because Haydn was doing his job and carrying out his employer's wishes.

In the 1770s, Prince Nikolaus became passionately fond of opera, and Haydn was obliged to rehearse and direct productions for Esterháza's purpose-built opera stage as well as its marionette theatre. He also composed a couple of dozen operas of his own. Today the average operagoer would be hard-pressed to name even one of Haydn's works. They are seldom performed and little regarded in comparison with Mozart's. You feel that Haydn's heart wasn't really in writing for the stage. But he did it because it was his job, and the influence it had on his other music was profound. Moments of recitative turn up in his piano sonatas and string quartets. The instruments are quite clearly meant to be speaking to us. More generally, though, the dramatic contrasts that characterise Haydn's non-dramatic music are without precedent. Even Carl Philipp Emanuel Bach, a dramatic composer if ever there was one, did not pack such bold contrasts into his instrumental and orchestral works. Haydn used extremes of dynamic — *forte, piano, forte, piano* — within a couple of bars. There are also dozens of examples, in all genres, of the music suddenly stopping in its tracks. Silence. Nothing. Then on it goes. Sometimes these moments are humorous — the composer's command of comic timing was always good, and the silences invariably take us by surprise — but sometimes we find ourselves staring into a terrifying void. Haydn's most dramatic music was in his non-vocal works.

As the composer's expressive language expanded, so did the level of ambition in his symphonies and quartets. The works became longer; three movements became four movements. Musical structures became increasingly complex, and the newly evolved first-movement form of the 'classical style' epitomised the era and its music. It is worth dwelling on matters of form. In hindsight we can see that what we usually refer to as 'sonata form' dominated the music of this period, and yet I am not convinced that Haydn, in spite of his major contribution to it, would have known quite what we mean by the expression.

Sonata form is mostly to be discerned in the first movements of Classical sonatas, string quartets and symphonies. Old-fashioned music appreciation courses and the more technical program notes served up at classical concerts describe it in terms of 'subjects'. There is a first subject (a theme or a group of themes), followed by a contrasting second subject. The statement of these themes is usually called the 'exposition'. Then the two themes fight it out in a 'development' section, in the process pulling themselves apart a bit; finally, in the 'recapitulation', there is usually a degree of resolution — it might be triumphant or not, but it will feel like a homecoming. None of that is exactly wrong, but the terms and descriptions always trouble me because they ignore the fundamental matter of harmony.

In the late eighteenth century, music was going through one of its rather harmonically simple and direct phases. (You could argue that a lot of composers are in another such phase at present.) After the dense polyphony of the High Renaissance and the tortured chromaticism of a lot of late-baroque compositions, the clean classical lines of diatonic harmony seemed attractive and modern and they fitted the prevailing mood of the Enlightenment. Diatonic harmony, as its name suggests, is bipolar. The tonic or home key has an (almost) equal and opposite pole in the dominant. If the tonic is C, the dominant will be G. Men and women of the Enlightenment enjoyed such clearly delineated music, where everything was boldly laid out. The mysteries of the world could be understood by reason, based on experience; to debate such matters, in a rigorous, balanced way, was the height of civilisation: on the one hand this (the tonic), on the other hand that (the dominant). Diatonic harmony belongs to such a reasonable world, and the first and second 'subjects' we so often hear about were a way of making the harmonic polarities clearer. They were also a way of clarifying the musical argument.

Whether Haydn understood this is not clear to me. Haydn does not seem to me to be one of history's great intellectuals. He composed music according to the style of the day and expanded that style in response to the circumstances of his employment. As it happened, his employer's devotion to God and to opera allowed the composer to enrich his music with levels of seriousness and drama that perfectly accorded with the Enlightenment's own devotion to balanced debate and reasoned rhetoric.

But another aspect to Haydn's music suggests that he had some ideas of his own. His music might have been composed for the old Austro-Hungarian aristocracy and for the new bourgeoisie of Paris and London, but it looked far beyond them. Even holed up in Esterháza, Haydn was aware of a world — a musical world — outside its front door. His own beginnings as the son of a wheelwright had been humble enough. Into Haydn's symphonies and sonatas and string quartets stream demotic sounds of bagpipes and fiddles, drones and drums. At the end of the first of his 'Paris' symphonies (No. 82), the Freemasons were treated to a bear-dance the like of which wouldn't turn up in the concert hall again until Béla Bartók came along. In the last of the London symphonies (No. 104), a prominent drone begins the last movement, so that for decades it was usually known as the symphony *mit dem Dudelsack* ('the symphony with the bagpipes'). But there are yet more startling examples of such 'peasant invasions'. Symphonies Nos. 67 and 88 both have their third movement minuets waylaid by the arrival of quite violently disruptive drones. Suddenly we are listening to folk music; the orchestra has turned into a giant hurdy-gurdy. In No. 88, the metre of the music is simultaneously disrupted. Even after Stravinsky, it is still a jolt to hear it.

When Gustav Mahler claimed to have composed the whole world in his third symphony, he was taking found musical objects into his massive ninety-minute work in order to have them comment ironically or affectionately on the human condition. The fanfare, the march, the *ländler*, the children's song: they are summoned up to throw stark light into our daily reality, maybe even into our souls. But it was Mahler's light. And it was Mahler's 'whole world', not yours or mine.

Haydn, however, while refining the very form that Mahler, a century later, would take and personalise, and while maintaining a gruelling schedule just to keep up with the demand for his music, managed to open the doors of his art to the world around him. The great philosophers of the Enlightenment and the gypsy fiddler; the dance and the debate; the rich man in his castle, the poor man at his gate: if you want to know what life was really like in late-eighteenth-century Europe, listen to Haydn.

Beethoven's song and dance

Perhaps five or six times, a piece of music that I have composed has turned up in the same concert as a work by Ludwig van Beethoven. It gives you pause for thought. For nearly two centuries, Beethoven has been considered history's greatest composer, and having your name appear alongside his in a concert program can seem a lot like impertinence. But there is also a level of sheer incongruity involved here. That any modern composer's name should appear alongside Beethoven's suggests that the music of each has something in common. Does it? What really is the relevance of Beethoven, who died in 1827, to a composer of the twenty-first century?

For his contemporaries, as for later nineteenth-century composers, his relevance was immediate and potentially daunting. Beethoven's music — the very *idea* of Beethoven's music — was unavoidable. Schubert and Brahms were just two of the major composers of that period to find themselves occasional victims of creative paralysis thanks to the long shadow cast by his figure. Berlioz was such a fan that he reputedly attempted to stab an audience member he had overheard criticising Beethoven's fifth symphony.

'Beethoven opened a new world of music for me,' Berlioz said, 'as Shakespeare had revealed a new universe of poetry.' It is still a useful comparison.

Beethoven is relevant to the twenty-first century in the same way Shakespeare is relevant. I do not mean to imply that he speaks to us down the ages of the human condition, or even that he was a purveyor of eternal truths, though I suppose both those statements may be true; and I am certainly not proposing, in some cheap, postmodern manner, that Beethoven is cool. Far from it. Indeed, I will be so *uncool* as to suggest that Beethoven's relevance, like Shakespeare's, is simply his greatness. Greatness, I think, is always relevant. Moreover, Beethoven is great in precisely the same way that Shakespeare is great, and for many of the same reasons. It is partly to do with range, partly with technique, and partly with sheer creative audacity.

Neither artist ever produced what you might call a typical work. You sense a clean slate at the outset of a piece of music by Beethoven or a play by Shakespeare. Anything might happen, you feel. This is not to suggest that earlier artists always wrote to a formula. Before Beethoven, Haydn and Mozart found almost infinite variety within their chosen musical forms. And it is important to emphasise that these forms arose from the prevailing musical styles of the day, and particularly the harmonic conventions; they were never sets of rules handed down from some higher musical authority. Nevertheless, although Haydn and Mozart's individual sonatas and string quartets, symphonies and concertos are distinctive and memorable, it is broadly true that their quartets and symphonies are in four movements and last around thirty minutes while their sonatas and concertos usually have three movements and are a bit shorter. Even allowing for the many exceptions (if you play every repeat in Mozart's last symphony, you can probably drag it out to forty minutes), there was nothing prior to Beethoven, in terms of design or intention or length or, most notably, sound, that was the equivalent of his third symphony, the *Eroica*.

Beethoven's nine symphonies — and it is significant that he composed ninety-eight fewer of them than Haydn — are all independent creations. Like Shakespeare's plays, they are worlds of their own. Take their opening bars. Beethoven's Symphony No. 1, remarkably, begins with a perfect cadence, the very gesture that had *ended* nearly every piece of classical music up to that moment: it is an elegant slap in the face, delivered with perfect comic timing. The second symphony has perhaps the most standard classical opening of a Beethoven symphony, a big unison D (the piece is in D major) complete with drum stroke, leading to a slow introduction such as Haydn or Mozart might have written. But with the *Eroica* we are somewhere else entirely. The key of the symphony is stated twice, a simple *staccato* chord — *thwack, thwack* — as though to call the audience to attention, and then without ceremony the first theme appears. And it is like no theme you have heard before. Indeed, the word 'theme' is almost too good for it as it merely delineates the notes of that same E flat chord before collapsing, apparently defeated, onto a dissonant D flat. This is heroic? Well, no. But what follows, taking the best part of an hour to play itself out, surely is. Something one learns early on in listening to Beethoven, is that this was a composer who could take apparently unpromising material and transform it into magnificent music. Shakespeare could do this with his characters, even with his heroes. Think of Coriolanus who grows, during the course of the drama that bears his name, from a petulant and frankly unattractive thug into one of theatre's most complex tragic figures. (Beethoven's *Coriolan* overture, incidentally, has nothing whatever to do with Shakespeare's *Coriolanus*, but was composed for a play on the same subject by Heinrich Joseph von Collin.)

After the *Eroica*, the later symphonies of Beethoven lead us into more rarefied worlds. The slow introduction of the fourth seems particularly mysterious even now, as it meanders chromatically across some desolate landscape, leading who knows where. In contrast, the famous opening bars of the fifth symphony have become a kind of modern cliché, which means, of course, that today we tend to miss their real significance. As with the *Eroica*, the symphony starts abruptly, but this time the 'shut-up-and-listen' gesture does not usher in a theme — it *is* the theme. And for those who had heard the work's predecessor, it must have been an especially disturbing theme because the opening salvo of the fifth symphony is a belated, violent reply to the opening notes of the fourth.

Just as the fifth symphony announces its tersely dramatic intentions in its opening bar, so the sixth instantly speaks of the countryside. It is not so much the familiar, tripping melody of the violins that would have alerted Beethoven's audiences to the music's pastoral intentions, but the underpinning accompaniment of the violas and cellos. They simply sustain the interval of an open fifth, and this drone would immediately have suggested to the composer's contemporaries a kind of music from beyond the concert hall: fiddles, hurdy-gurdies and bagpipes. In a word, shepherds. The seventh symphony has the longest of Beethoven's slow introductions. It seems not only to quote from the finale of the *Pastoral* symphony, but also to offer a melodic premonition of the nineteenth-century dance party that is about to ensue. By contrast, the eighth symphony (which continues the dancing) jumps straight in. The ninth, and last, of Beethoven's symphonies has perhaps the most remarkable beginning of all, being simultaneously a classical slow introduction and a piece of early-Romantic mood-setting, while also managing to foreshadow the work's first subject.

And that is just the beginnings. And just the symphonies. The same point about stylistic heterogeneity might have been made with reference to the piano concertos or the violin sonatas or, at rather greater length, the string quartets or piano sonatas. As the scholar and pianist Charles Rosen points out, 'the Beethoven sonatas constituted the first body of substantial serious works for the piano adequate for performance in large concert halls seating hundreds'. By the time of his death in 1827, the public piano recital had yet to be invented — Franz Liszt achieved this a decade later — but Beethoven's sonatas quickly became staples, and one of the reasons, surely, was their sheer variety. Significantly, they varied not only in style and content but also in their technical difficulty. Of the 'Hammerklavier', Rosen reports that Carl Czerny told Beethoven, 'There is a lady in Vienna ... who has been practising your B flat sonata for a month, and she still can't play the beginning'.

The stylistic range in Beethoven's music — the range of gesture, of emotion, of mood — seems to me primarily dramatic. It is not, of course, a conventional sort of theatrical drama. The characters in these symphonies and sonatas, their actions and interactions, are abstract. Beethoven did not invent this approach to instrumental music, it grew naturally from the musical idiom of the day, which emphasised contrast and struggle (sonata form) as much as balance. But Beethoven took things very much further than anyone before him. It is surely relevant that his one genuine opera, *Fidelio*, caused him endless problems. In no sense abstract, this was drama about people and ideas, and the fact that he composed four separate overtures for it gives an indication of the struggle it became. In the end, it seems to me, *Fidelio* is little more than the sum of its parts, notwithstanding the fact that a few of those parts (the quartet in Act 1, for instance, and the chorus of prisoners) contain music of striking beauty. But the abstract dramas of the symphonies, sonatas and quartets are invariably successful. Just as Shakespeare's gifts as a dramatist were inseparable from his gifts as a poet (the way his words actually sound), so Beethoven's music is fundamentally linked to his dramatic sense, and part of that musical drama involved taking found objects and transforming them.

When Haydn and Mozart included minuets in their works, which they did very frequently, they brought their own personality to the dance. Nonetheless, their treatment of the minuet-template is generally 'in style' while its presence in a symphony or string quartet harks back to the dance movements that comprised the suites and partitas of the baroque era. The rustic German dance that features in the *Danza alla tedesca* movement of Beethoven's string quartet in B flat, Op. 130, is a little different. Here, it seems, the composer is quoting. The effect, I suppose, is similar to Haydn's use of gypsy music and Mozart's of Turkish, but it is not exactly the same. Haydn and Mozart were playing musical dress-ups; Beethoven wasn't.

Beethoven's German dance comes in the middle of a big piece with six movements, the last of which, before the composer's publisher got cold feet, was the massive *Grosse Fuge*, adding nearly twenty minutes of unusually dense and fervent music to a quartet that had already been playing for half an hour. The *Danza alla tedesca*, innocent and unsophisticated in the midst of all that world-weary melancholy and restless striving, has a dramatic function in Beethoven's quartet; it is playing a role. The obvious comparison is not with the minuets of Haydn and Mozart or even with those composers' exotic 'world music' appropriations. The comparison is with the symphonies of Gustav Mahler: the off-stage brass bands, the funeral marches, the cowbells, the fanfares and, above all, the *ländlers*, those peasant precursors of the waltz. Beethoven and Mahler (and, for that matter, Charles Ives) took everyday musical objects in order to transform them and to allow the objects to transform the musical structures into which they had been dragged, as it were, off the street. Popular dance is thus 'ennobled', but more importantly it also offers a commentary, critical or ironic, on the bourgeois surroundings in which it finds itself.

The grandest example of dance transforming sonata form in Beethoven's output is the seventh symphony, the one Wagner famously dubbed 'the apotheosis of the dance'. This symphony is equally exceptional in that, although each movement is evidently a dance of some sort, none is a minuet or a gavotte or any other type of dance from Beethoven's time and place. The great Beethoven scholar and biographer, Maynard Solomon, taking his lead from Czerny, has gone to great lengths in his book on late Beethoven to prove that the rhythms in the seventh symphony are the same as those of classical Greek poetry. As Czerny had already shown, there are certainly useful comparisons to be found. But I do not believe Wagner's ears often let him down, and I'm sure they didn't on this occasion. What Wagner responded to in

Beethoven's seventh symphony was its corporeality. This is a dance symphony.

So where did the rhythms come from? The structure of the third movement is closer to a *gallop* than to a conventional scherzo. The *gallop* would be the next big Parisian dance craze, but not for another decade and a half, so if Beethoven had any model in mind for his movement, it must have been the antique German predecessor of the *gallop* known as the *Hopser*. This is a frankly arcane source. As for the glorious second movement, the only dance steps one might convincingly fit to that are those of a pavan, the rather stately, two-beats-in-a-bar dance from the sixteenth century that often kept company with a matching galliard in a triple metre. Again, one wonders where Beethoven was getting this from. It's hard to imagine him poring over old manuscripts. Was he perhaps simply inventing these metres? Certainly the first and last sections of the seventh symphony, relentless, dance-till-you-drop movements without precedent in symphonic music, are equally lacking in precedent on the dance floor. The seventh symphony transfigures all these dance rhythms, pushing them relentlessly, the effect being not unlike techno or trance music — triphop, I suppose, in the case of the second movement. The invention in Beethoven's symphony is primarily rhythmic and harmonic, rather than melodic (not such a surprise with this composer), but the end result is a sort of rhythmically induced ecstasy. You begin to imagine tunes that aren't there. In the second movement in particular, the nearest thing to a real tune is, in truth, a rather limp countermelody to some unstated theme, but Beethoven — once again transcending the mundane — makes it seem inspired.

If you read some of the attempts by Beethoven's contemporaries and successors to describe this music (Solomon has thoughtfully gathered some in his famous biography of the composer) you encounter wilder and wilder claims. Berlioz thought the first movement was a peasant dance, while the musicologist and statesman Wilhelm von Lenz considered it a second pastoral symphony (and I think he had a point). Among Beethoven's biographers, Ludwig Nohl imagined a festive gathering of knights, Paul Bekker a 'bacchic orgy' and A. B. Marx a warrior people's wedding celebration. Solomon himself, evidently amused by these extravagant attempts to construe Beethoven's meaning in the seventh symphony, is very keen to link that work to the eighth.

'They exist in a festal paradise,' Solomon writes, 'outside of time and history, untouched by mortality.' And it is perfectly true. The eighth takes up where the seventh leaves off. With no slow introduction, not even a couple of chords as in the *Eroica*, Beethoven's eighth symphony plunges headlong into yet another dance. Again the only model one can call to mind, and it may or may not have been conscious on the part of the composer, is from the sixteenth century. The first movement of Beethoven's Symphony No. 8 is the galliard to the seventh's pavan. Performed at the tempo Beethoven stipulates, it quickly becomes as manic as any of the dance movements from the preceding symphony, the glorious melody stripped away until only a fragment of the jagged rhythm remains, a repetitious, stuck-in-the-groove moment as stark as the most minimal dance club track.

Melody, you begin to realise, is essential to Beethoven's music and to its dramatic agenda. It is as important when it is not there — for example, in the opening movements of the fifth symphony and the first *Razumovsky* quartet (Op. 59 No. 1) — as when it is the very heart of the musical matter. In the late piano sonatas and string quartets there is an irrepressible lyricism. Sometimes it is suggested that long melodies are absent from Beethoven's earlier works, so much are linear forms such as variations and fugues a part of his late music. But this is untrue. One need think only of the *Pathétique* sonata, which had certainly been composed by 1799 and is therefore an early piece. There is hardly a lovelier melody in all of Beethoven's work than the central *Adagio*. Following his initial lessons with Haydn, Beethoven had studied with Johann Georg Albrechtsberger, a Viennese teacher famous for his insistence on counterpoint, so Beethoven also knew how to write fugues from an early age. And of course there are sets of variations from every stage in his composing career. The finale of the *Eroica* employs variation form.

And yet it is true that the later music is obsessed with lyricism. Just as dance threatened the fabric of symphonic form in the seventh and eighth symphonies, so song invades and subverts the late sonatas and string quartets. Beethoven never abandoned sonata form, and the hallmarks of the style — the statement of themes, their development and later recapitulation — continued to be at the heart of his music, but not only were non-standard forms admitted to his works, they were also increasingly identified as such. The piano sonatas Opp. 110 and 111 contain movements headed *Arioso* and *Arietta;* in the string quartet Op. 130 comes the famous *Cavatina*. These are all operatic terms; they refer to singing. Again, one cannot help but recall the struggle with *Fidelio*.

Fugues erupt in the development sections of the sonatas Opp. 101, 106, 110 and 111. A furious fugue originally ended the quartet Op. 130 and another, much calmer, fugue begins the quartet Op. 131. There is fugal writing in the finale of the ninth symphony. And then there are all those variations. Both the sonatas Opp. 109 and 111 contain sets of variations (I would want to argue that the whole of Op. 109 is really a set of variations on a theme that is only properly stated at the beginning of the finale) and so do the string quartets Opp. 127 and 135. And of course there is the *Diabelli* Variations. This is not only the longest set of variations Beethoven ever composed, it is also one of his most significant pieces. Part of its significance is that it finally unites song and dance.

Anton Diabelli's undistinguished theme (another sow's ear made into a silk purse) is a waltz, and the structure of the dance itself is as subject to variation as its harmony and melody. In the very first variation, Beethoven turns the waltz into a march. This is a piece about transformation and it makes use of all the concerns of the composer's late music: the penultimate variation is even a fugue. In this work, the serious and the trivial meet and coexist. Banality and profundity rub shoulders. Jokes abound. For no good reason, Don Giovanni's sidekick Leporello makes a guest appearance humming an aria from Mozart's opera. And yet some of these variations are among the composer's most sublime creations. Because of the nature of variation form (here there are thirty-three variations in something like an hour), the changes of pace and mood come thick and fast, often without warning. The *Diabelli Variations* is at once the most abstract and most lifelike drama Beethoven ever composed.

Ultimately what continues to astonish us about Beethoven is his ambition. No composer has ever reached for more. Beethoven set new standards, not just for music but also for composers. No wonder his colleagues and successors felt daunted. No wonder Brahms took fourteen years over his first symphony, completing it only at the age of forty-three. If he or she stops to think about it, the twenty-first century composer has precisely the same problem with Beethoven as the nineteenth-century composer: the problem of living up to the example he set.

The dramatic imagination of Hector Berlioz

However one draws up the history of Western music, it is hard to make Hector Berlioz fit neatly into it. In many ways the most French of composers, he does not even seem to belong to French music. He owes virtually nothing to the likes of Lully and Rameau before him, and neither does he point the way to Debussy and Ravel. If anything, Berlioz's influences (both those on him and his on others) are all German. Beethoven was his hero, and Wagner, one suspects, might not have been quite the composer he was without Berlioz. But even that is hard to prove.

Berlioz's greatest formal innovations are so idiosyncratic that they resist imitation. His harmonic language remains the subject of debate: was he a true original or was he just clumsy? There is really only one area in which agreement is general: Berlioz had a brilliant ear for orchestral effects, and few composers since have failed to benefit from his example. Even if it took until the twentieth century to appreciate the fact, it would be no exaggeration to say that Berlioz, more than any other single figure, invented the modern symphony orchestra.

Berlioz wrote a book on the subject of orchestration, and it is a volume that all composers since have consulted. There is a fabulous sonic imagination at work here, as though Berlioz was incapable of thinking of a group of pitches without hearing them played in his mind's ear on this or that instrument. He was the first composer (but certainly not the last) for whom the quality of a sound sometimes mattered more than the actual notes.

A few of Berlioz's most famous orchestral effects seem, on the face of it, little more than grandiloquence. Continually seeking to expand the forces available to him, he fantasised about bringing together all the musicians in Paris. He describes an orchestra of 467 players, including 120 violins, sixteen horns, thirty harps and thirty pianos, twelve pairs of antique cymbals, six glockenspiels, six triangles and four Turkish crescents (bell trees). This has nothing to do with extra volume; at least, nothing much. What interests Berlioz here is the possibility of new sonorities. He imagines taking the thirty harps and 120 violins (all playing *pizzicato*) and turning them into a giant 934-string harp; he advocates combining the pianos with the glockenspiels, triangles, antique cymbals and Turkish crescents, thus producing a 'metallic percussion orchestra for joyful and brilliant accents'.

There is something undeniably megalomaniacal about all this, but it is always the sound of the music — and often the sound of the music in *space* — that Berlioz is concerned with. In his Requiem of 1837, requiring only slightly more modest forces than those just described (it employs sixteen kettledrums, for instance), the physical placing of instruments is important. The orchestra's extremely large brass contingent (twelve trumpets, sixteen trombones, six tubas) is divided into four brass choirs and then distributed about the performance space, providing an array of antiphonal effects. Even if Berlioz knew of Gabrieli's and Monteverdi's similar experiments in Venice's St Mark's Cathedral over 200 years before — and that seems unlikely — he trumps their effects many times over in his *Grande messe des morts*.

It is grandiloquent beyond words, but Berlioz was at least as concerned with the tiny details of his orchestral sounds as with their potential splendour. In the *Hostias* of the Requiem, a delicate four-note chord represents the Host itself. Berlioz allocates the lowest of these notes to eight trombones playing (quietly) in unison, while three solo flutes play the other notes. It is orchestrational insanity, and no other composer, before or since, would have dreamt it up. But it works. The chord gleams. Musical transubstantiation!

It is often the quietest moments in Berlioz's music that are the most telling. He might have composed no chamber music (beyond some juvenilia), but there is scarcely a lack of intimacy in even his largest-scale works. Often these moments are dramatic, arriving suddenly after a big noise. For example, in the Funeral March Berlioz devised for the final scene of *Hamlet*, the relentless beating of a dozen side-drums reaches its climax in a deafening volley of off-stage musketry. This is followed by a silence that is eventually filled by plaintive wisps of melody from the lower strings, the funereal tattoo replaced by a distant tolling gong.

Berlioz's music, it should by now be clear, is intrinsically dramatic, and there is a dramatic rationale behind nearly all his orchestral innovations. Similarly, it is drama that guides and shapes his musical structures, big and small. For example, when he writes a fugue — which is rather often — it is not for simply musical reasons. Neither is there anything academic about his approach to the form (indeed, Berlioz's fugues often unravel soon after they begin). Fugal writing in Berlioz's music is symbolic of dramatic movement. A fast fugue, such as the one that opens the 'dramatic symphony' *Roméo et Juliette*, is a chase, and here it stands for a skirmish between warring families. The more gentle fugue that starts the second part of *L'Enfance du Christ* is also a chase of sorts, as the Holy Family makes its sedate escape via donkey to Egypt.

This dramatic sensibility even shapes Berlioz's melodic writing, which is nearly as distinctive as his orchestration. Take Romeo's lonely theme in *Roméo et Juliette*. A sighing figure (that would later inspire the opening phrases of Wagner's *Tristan und Isolde*) gives way to a melodic line which meanders forlornly. But then so does Romeo. The distant strains of the Capulets' ball invade his reverie and lure him on, giving him purpose (and giving his melody a regular metre and a proper accompaniment). Finally, as he enters the ball, the two musics collide, the long notes of Romeo's theme bestriding the flashing commotion of the Capulets' dance band. Musically it is at once dazzling and dangerous. And of course, by this point in the story, Romeo himself is pretty wired.

Or consider the famous *idée fixe*, the motto theme that crops up in every movement of *Symphonie fantastique*. I can think of few melodic lines before it — not even in late Beethoven — that are so free. It is very hard to pin this melody down, in part because it is rhythmically irregular, but mostly because Berlioz has managed to compose a melodic line that implies no particular harmony. This is usually considered one of the composer's weaknesses, and it is true that Berlioz's harmonic sense was not at all on the same level as his ability in orchestration. Too often you can hear how he has added chords to an existing melody rather than have the melody propose its own harmony. And this application of harmony is often slapdash, betraying Berlioz's tendency to pick out the chords on his guitar. It is a weakness, to be sure. But it is a weakness in a great composer, and part of Berlioz's greatness was his ability to turn his poor ear for harmony to his advantage. It is, after all, entirely appropriate that the *idée fixe* should seem disembodied, floating in from another world: that is its function in this work. For Berlioz, content always gave shape to form, and nowhere more so than in that great warhorse of the repertoire, *Symphonie fantastique*.

The status of *Symphonie fantastique* is entirely justified. It may not be perfect — no art is, and Berlioz's music is amongst the most flawed great art ever created — but after more than 170 years, the *Fantastique* has retained its power to astonish listeners. Berlioz was just twenty-six when he composed this piece, his Opus 14, in 1830. Subtitled 'episode from the life of an artist' and inspired by Berlioz's hot-headed passion for the Irish Shakespearean actress Harriet Smithson, the symphony describes the moments of torture and ecstasy experienced so forcefully by this most self-dramatising of composers. Berlioz had first seen Smithson as Ophelia in a touring production of *Hamlet* and he became obsessed with her. In *Symphonie fantastique*, she is represented by the *idée fixe*.

In the first movement, the 'Artist' sees and instantly falls in love with the object of his desire. He cannot get her out of his mind. The *idée fixe* dominates this movement. In the subsequent movements the artist attends a glittering ball, but spies his beloved (cue *idée fixe*); he retires to the country, but the memory of her will not leave him (there it is again). He takes an overdose of opium, but it only makes matters worse: he dreams he has murdered her and is to be executed for his crimes (just before the blade comes down, he hears the theme); he winds up at a witches' sabbath where the image of his beloved mocks him, the *idée fixe*, once so ineffable, now transformed into a hideously perky little tune suitable for a boxwood clarinet.

The five-movement scheme owes something to Beethoven's *Pastoral* symphony, and there is even the suggestion of a few borrowings in the nature music of the third movement, but this should not detract from the staggering originality of the work.

This was a *symphony?* At its premiere, later in 1830, the 'March to the Scaffold' had to be encored, and the work as a whole was received with great enthusiasm. The following year Berlioz produced its sequel, one of the most startling creations in all nineteenth-century music. And here lies a paradox. For while everyone knows *Symphonie fantastique*, knowledge of its companion piece is limited to connoisseurs, musicologists and Berlioz devotees.

The basic conceit is this. After *Symphonie fantastique* is played, the audience leaves the auditorium. On its return, a curtain has dropped and the orchestra has vanished from view. Now an actor steps forward. It is the 'Artist' himself, still groggy from all that opium, but alive — returned to life. His name is Lélio, and its similarity to Berlioz is not a coincidence.

Lélio (or *The Return to Life*) Op. 14b takes up the story where the *Fantastique* left off. The artist speaks directly to the audience, his still-addled mind free-associating images from his life and from his dream. He thinks of his friend Horatio. As luck would have it, Horatio is a singer and we hear his voice, accompanied by piano, floating out from behind the curtain. He is singing a song about a fisherman. The words are Goethe's. A little later, Lélio suddenly announces: 'I'd like to go to Calabria ... even if it meant being a ... a ... BRIGAND!' Lélio is semi-delirious, remember, so he is liable to say pretty much anything. Before you can question the somewhat strained logic in all this, a chorus of brigands has erupted behind the curtain (yes, there is a chorus there too).

And on it goes. Finally, in a quite literal *coup de théâtre*, the curtain rises to reveal chorus, soloists, orchestra and conductor. They are about to rehearse — to *rehearse*, mark you — a musical fantasy on Shakespeare's play *The Tempest*, which Lélio has composed. And Lélio is on hand with advice for everyone: 'Watch the conductor ... The singers shouldn't hold their music books in front of their faces ... Don't lag behind the beat.' Berlioz/Lélio's 'Fantasia on *The Tempest*' contains what is probably the first use of a piano in a symphony orchestra, but with all else that is going on, this scarcely registers.

According to J. H. Elliot in his 1938 monograph on Berlioz, '*Lélio* must be the craziest work ever sketched out by a composer not actually insane'. Elliot's book is refreshingly candid about the shortcomings of a composer the author greatly admires, but his judgment on *Lélio* still strikes me as harsh. *Lélio* is an important work, well before its time. One thinks of Fellini's film *Orchestra Rehearsal*, and of those works by the twentieth-century Italian composer Luciano Berio — *Sinfonia*, *Opera* and *Recital* — in which the performers discuss the performance they are giving. One thinks of post-modernist frame-breaking moments when performers address audiences. There is still nothing quite like *Lélio*.

One of the reasons it strikes me as such an impressive achievement is that *Lélio* is, in fact, a ragbag of discarded music from the composer's bottom drawer. The fisherman's song and the chorus of brigands were leftovers from abandoned projects. Even the 'Fantasia on *The Tempest*' already existed. For that matter, both the even-numbered movements of *Symphonie fantastique* had been composed in advance of the idea for the symphony, and this explains why, in each case, the *idée fixe* arrives only in the closing bars and very much in quotation marks: it had not been part of the composer's original plan. And yet neither half of Opus 14 sounds like the patchwork it actually is. What binds the patches together is Berlioz's unerring sense of musical drama.

In 1852, Richard Wagner wrote to Franz Liszt regarding his concern for their mutual colleague: 'If ever a musician needed a poet it is Berlioz, and it is his misfortune that he always adapts his poet to his own musical whim, arranging now Shakespeare, now Goethe, to suit his own purpose. He needs a poet to fill him through and through, a poet driven by ecstasy to violate him, and who is to him what a man is to a woman.'

Of course these could only be Wagner's words. It is not so much the confident, boys-will-be-boys attitude to sexual domination that gives him away — like his anti-Semitism, Wagner shared his sexual politics with most of the rest of Europe's bourgeois intelligentsia. No, it is the size of the ego. As the poet James Fenton has reminded us, the poet whom Wagner had in mind for the ravishing of Berlioz was Wagner himself. Wagner felt his unused operatic scenario *Wieland the Blacksmith* would leave the Frenchman panting in musical submission. It would, of course, be impossible to imagine Wagner advancing this argument about music submitting to poetry had he not been the author of his own librettos. He could advocate the poetic violation of Berlioz and all other composers because when it came to his own case something closer to auto-violation was involved, Wagner-the-composer lying back and thinking of Germany while Wagner-the-poet had his wicked way.

But all that aside, Wagner was doubly wrong in his thesis. Berlioz had plenty of poets in his life and he by no means always adapted them to his own will. He was well acquainted with the work of Virgil and Goethe, Byron and Walter Scott, Théophile Gautier and Thomas More, and the names of all these writers turn up in the composer's catalogue of works, either as providers of texts or offerers of inspiration. But the poet who ravished Berlioz and whose influence is felt in his music from start to finish is Shakespeare. ('Ô Shakespeare! Shakespeare!' Lélio exclaims, swooning.)

The affair began the night Berlioz first saw Harriet Smithson. This was certainly value for money in the theatre. Not only was Harriet up there on stage (he would later marry her), but also his reaction to *Hamlet* was one of the most high-profile examples of 'Stendhal's syndrome' in history. (The nineteenth-century French author Stendhal described how he was overcome with emotion followed by feelings of dizziness on first viewing Giotto's frescos in Santa Croce in Florence.) Shakespeare ravished Berlioz again and again. In his rather small catalogue of works, we find not only *Roméo et Juliette*, a *King Lear* overture, the *Hamlet* funeral march, the 'Fantasia on *The Tempest*', and a song, 'The Death of Ophelia', but also the composer's final opera, *Béatrice et Bénédict*, which was based on *Much Ado About Nothing*.

But the other reason Wagner was wrong is that he failed to understand the nature of Berlioz's musical mind — its dramatic nature. He might have been happy to have them ravish him, but afterwards Berlioz was quick to put Shakespeare and Virgil and Byron to work. Writing to the Princess Sayn-Wittgenstein in 1856 in reply to a letter complimenting Berlioz on his libretto for *Les Troyens* ('The Trojans'), the composer thanks her for her comments, then proceeds gently to upbraid her. The libretto, he writes, 'is beautiful because it is Virgil; it is striking because it is Shakespeare. I am only an interloper: I have ransacked the gardens of two geniuses, and cut a swathe of flowers to make a couch for music, where god grant she may not perish overcome by the fragrance.'

There wasn't much chance of that. Berlioz's attitude to poetry was actually the opposite of Wagner's, and he knew it even if Wagner did not.

'The great difficulty throughout,' Berlioz wrote to the princess, 'is to find the *musical* form — the form without which music does not exist, or exists only as the abject slave of the word. There lies Wagner's crime: he wants to dethrone music and reduce it to expressive accents.'

For precisely this reason, Berlioz's stage works, his operas, are not the greatest works of this musical dramatist. Certainly, *Les Troyens* and *Béatrice et Bénédict* contain some of his finest music, but structurally — *dramatically* — these works adhere to the recitative/aria/chorus template. They are formulaic, old hat. Berlioz's most original works — and his most *dramatic* works — were, like Beethoven's, composed for the concert hall. Here his musical structures were as unprecedented as the sounds he coaxed from his orchestras, and they remain unique.

The honesty of
Johannes Brahms

I am not much of a singer in the shower; instead, I sort of inwardly hum to myself. I do it walking along the street, too, and cutting the grass or digging in the backyard. Virtually any sort of mindless activity sparks this internal humming, but it was in the shower that I first noticed it was Brahms. There would have been nothing odd about this except that I noticed it twice, a couple of days apart, and on the second occasion, although it was still Brahms, it was a different piece.

I began to keep a half-hearted account of this apparently trivial phenomenon, until after a number of weeks — perhaps it was months — I realised I had enough Brahms pieces intermittently popping into my head to fill a boxed set of CDs. The second and third symphonies, the first of the string sextets, the Piano Concerto No. 1, the Violin Concerto, *A*

German Requiem: they had all had turned up, unbidden, while I was showering. There was other music, too, but Brahms's works were the most frequent visitors.

Let me be the first to admit that this looks slightly crazy: the humming itself, the preponderance of Brahms and, not least, my logging of the music all make me appear eccentric and obsessive. My reason for vouchsafing such embarrassing personal information is that it forced me to think about the music, and, in the process, I learned some things about Brahms. When I say that I found myself humming these pieces, naturally I don't mean the entire pieces. The shortest of these works lasts more than half an hour, and they are all in several movements. No, in each case I found myself humming a particular theme. I thought about this and began to realise that they were all second subjects of first movements, except for the theme from *A German Requiem* which was the second subject of the second movement ('All flesh is grass' — not an inappropriate sentiment for the shower).

The harmonic structure of a classical sonata form first movement, as already discussed, is usually delineated by the presence of a first subject (a theme or set of themes) in the home key and a second subject (theme or themes) in the dominant key, which is a fifth higher. In order to make this distinction clear, the first and second subjects tend to be rather different in character. Often enough, the first subject will have a bold, strongly rhythmic nature with maybe a touch of belligerence, while the second subject will possess what the politically incorrect music teachers of my youth used to call feminine characteristics — it will be more flowing and graceful, more lyrical. Brahms's music offers plenty of good examples, not least in my shower pieces, and the more I thought about the second-subject themes that kept occurring to me, the more I realised that they shared some other characteristics too.

This composer's attitude to harmony was considerably more classical than that of his contemporary Wagner. For one thing, Brahms seldom leaves his listeners in any doubt what key his music is in, and many of his tunes emerge, with surprising simplicity, from the delineation of that harmony; often a melody is little more than the rippling of an arpeggio. In the Piano Concerto No. 1, for example, the brass fanfare that concludes the first subject group of themes turns into a touchingly poignant second-subject figure for the piano. Really, it is little more than the rocking back and forth of the key note and its dominant (in this instance, a fourth lower instead of a fifth higher), the key note rising expressively to the tone above (the supertonic), the interval then gently expanding until the tune reaches its climax on the supertonic in the next octave.

To a non-musician, all this technical jargon might make it seem as though Brahms has achieved something impressively complex, but, on the contrary, the melody could scarcely be simpler. The composer has come up with a three-note wonder of a tune that slowly climbs the keyboard. The fact that the notes Brahms employs also so clearly define the harmony helps to make it memorable — so memorable that it will show up unbidden in the mind of someone daydreaming in the shower. But there is another aspect to this easy memorability, and it has to do with the way the notes are presented to us.

The gentle rocking motion of the melody is in triple time. Indeed, when I stopped to think about it, all my shower themes turned out to be in triple time. Some were actually waltzes (for example, the second subjects of Symphony No. 3 and the sextet), but even those that weren't explicitly 'Viennese' in this manner had leanings in that general direction. As the composer Robin Holloway has pointed out, the waltz for Brahms was both a form of normality and a representation of goodness. Even in his next-to-final musical utterance, the *Four Serious Songs*, the composer sets those well-known lines about love from St Paul's first letter to the Corinthians to a waltz tune, 'oleaginous yet beery' (Holloway's words), that strikes one as remarkably incongruous.

Until, that is, one thinks of Brahms's entire output and the place, in his music, of the waltz.

They are everywhere, these waltzes. They come in sets for piano solo, for piano duo, for two pianos. The famous *Liebeslieder* waltzes add voices in four parts. But they also show up, unannounced, in the symphonies and concertos and chamber music (not least in those second subjects), and even *A German Requiem*. After all, what, but a slow waltz, is that work's central vision of paradise, 'How lovely is thy dwelling place'? The waltz as a symbol of an eternal home: this is a very Brahmsian conceit. And so why, once we are able to see through a glass darkly, should it not be a waltz that we hear? Holloway puts it well and very reasonably: 'As the *jongleur* juggles before the Virgin because it's what he does naturally and best, so Brahms hymns Love in a waltz.'

There is something undeniably down-to-earth about Brahms's music, just as it seems there was about the composer himself. The scriptural texts he selected for *A German Requiem* avoid all mention of Jesus Christ. There are a few references to the 'Lord', but no names are mentioned. This so worried the organisers of the first performance at Bremen Cathedral on Good Friday 1868 that Brahms was prevailed upon to allow the performance, midway through his own work, of the aria 'I know that my redeemer liveth' from Handel's *Messiah*. It seems to me significant that Jesus was left out of it. The composer himself once suggested replacing the word 'German' in the title with 'humanist'. Now Brahms was no atheist — his Requiem was not, like Delius's Requiem, a godless work. But it was, above all, a work. Music, for Brahms, was a job, and like any other more or less conventional Lutheran, Brahms equated hard work with divine worship. Perhaps with a waltz in paradise at the end of the day.

Getting that work right was also important to Brahms. His early music in particular is full of pieces that are revised again and again. There is the string quintet in F minor that turned into a sonata for two pianos that eventually turned into the Piano Quintet. And there is the sonata for two pianos in D minor that very nearly became a symphony in D minor but actually ended up as the composer's first piano concerto —

the one with the three-note fanfare that turns into a waltz. Brahms began sketching his actual first symphony in Vienna in 1862, but completed it only in 1876. This self-critical artisan side of Brahms is something I confess I find very appealing, very honest. I think it is one of the reasons I trust his music. I also think it helps to explain his attitude to sonority.

Brahms's music is often described as drab, and it is true that poor performances can easily support this appellation. It is a criticism levelled, similarly, at his older contemporary and great supporter, Robert Schumann. It is probably fair to say that the art of orchestration, if not a nineteenth-century invention (Mozart, after all, was pretty good at it), was certainly a nineteenth-century obsession. Weber, Mendelssohn and Berlioz were all great innovators when it came to the alchemical possibilities of combining instrumental sounds. Wagner, let it not be forgotten, had the surest orchestral touch, bringing almost a secondary level of stage lighting to his music-dramas. For Mahler, even as the teenage composer of *Das klagende Lied*, orchestration often *was* drama. In the company of such contemporaries, Brahms can sometimes seem like a very dull dog.

But Brahms found precisely the right orchestral clothing for his music. It is doubtless fair to say that he favoured instrumental restraint — though try telling that to a pianist grappling with one of the 'accompaniments' to the clarinet or cello sonatas — but the chamber music and orchestral scores are nonetheless littered with orchestrational felicities, chiefly from wind instruments. Neither are his pieces devoid of innovation. The absence of violins from the orchestra in the first movement of *A German Requiem* might be a negative sort of drama, but it is still dramatic.

One of Brahms's later contemporaries — and one of his very greatest admirers — was Arnold Schoenberg (another underrated orchestrator). To the end of his life, Schoenberg quarried Brahms's music for examples in teaching composition, and he made his own orchestral arrangement of the Piano Quartet No. 1 in G minor. For most concertgoers this is hard to believe. The names of Brahms and Schoenberg seem to belong to different parts of the musical experience. You know where you are with Brahms; he is safe, strong and undemanding. Schoenberg is scary and confronting; you need a university education in order to appreciate his music, and if you say you actually like the stuff you must be either mad or lying. When, occasionally, Schoenberg's orchestration of the piano quartet turns up on a concert program, you can slice the audience's incomprehension with a breadknife. Can this be right? This piece sounds as straightforward as any other music by Brahms, as though it was orchestrated by the composer himself (with the arguable exception of the minor role allocated to a xylophone in the gypsy rondo at the end).

Why did Schoenberg admire Brahms so much? In 1933, the centenary of Brahms's birth (and fifty years after the death of Wagner), Schoenberg gave a lecture about the composer. He revised it in 1947, on the fiftieth anniversary of Brahms's death, and finally he published it as a long essay in his collection of writings, *Style and Idea*, in 1950. Entitled 'Brahms the Progressive', it sets out to demonstrate that in nearly every area of music — melody, harmony and rhythm (Schoenberg doesn't really discuss orchestration) — Brahms was as forward-thinking as Wagner. Schoenberg is at pains to dismiss the notion that Brahms was merely an academic and a classicist. And he makes many good points about the music, especially concerning its structural integrity and the way that motifs tend to proliferate in an almost organic manner.

But as one reads the essay, one starts to feel this author protests too much. In Brahms, I feel certain, Schoenberg had found a kindred spirit. The more Schoenberg pronounces Brahms to be a progressive, and the more he dismisses the perceived academicism and classicism, the more you realise these were precisely the things Schoenberg worried about in his own pieces. Schoenberg's music was deeply rooted in the past, however much it may have looked to the future, and Brahms was exactly the same.

It is very likely true that any great artist must look backwards as well as forwards. Schoenberg could not help himself, but Brahms did it quite consciously. He had almost a side career as an editor of baroque music by Francois Couperin, Handel and C. P. E. Bach. He was one of the first to attempt to disentangle Mozart's original work on his Requiem from the completions by his pupil, Franz Xavier Süssmayer. But this is not only evidence of an enthusiasm for musicology, it also shows us Brahms the hard worker, the professional, engaged in the business of music.

Thomas Shapcott captures this Brahms rather well in the first of three poems he calls 'Piano Pieces'. But there are other Brahmses here as well: not, perhaps, Schoenberg's 'progressive', but the Brahms who lived in the real world, the Brahms who said what he meant without the neon light of flashing orchestration, the Brahms who lifts our spirits, the trustworthy Brahms who brings reassurance.

Brahms

> *Cluttered with ash and coffee stains*
> *the old man's coat hangs on a nail,*
> *it is limp and shapeless, one pocket's torn*
> *and the others bulge out heavy and full.*
> *Even without him in the room*
> *the coat suggests his bulky form.*
> *Time's past and past since it was new,*
> *the cuff and the collar are worn quite through,*
> *but it keeps an old man safe and warm*
> *and will see him beyond this wintertime.*

If that seems perhaps too small a Brahms for you — or too cosy — it is worth returning to the figure of Brahms the worker and situating him firmly in his Lutheran surroundings. Work mattered to Brahms above all else, but the music that resulted from his labours serves to remind us that the Protestant work ethic is not simply a matter of duty or even worship; it is also the path to transcendence.

Sibelius's journey into silence

Jean Sibelius is one of the most fascinating composers of the twentieth century, almost as fascinating for the way in which his music was received as for the music itself. His career was fascinating too. And of course the career, the music and its reception are connected. In the end, I believe he was one of the great innovators, and that this, together with the fact that most of the world failed to recognise it, resulted in his retirement from composition three decades before his death.

The bare bones of Sibelius's life are these. He was born in 1865 into a Swedish-speaking Finnish family, but he was in no sense a prodigy. He had music lessons, as did many other children, but he did not begin with the violin until the age of fourteen. His first surviving attempt at composition dates from the following year. His rather protracted studies in composition took place in Helsinki, Berlin and Vienna. Finally, in 1892, by which time Sibelius was in his late twenties, he produced the piece that established his reputation, as it were, over night. This was the *Kullervo* symphony, a large-scale work for soprano and baritone soloists, choir and orchestra. The success of the work, based on episodes from the great Finnish epic poem the *Kalevala*, meant that the composer's name and music would remain firmly associated with Finnish nationalism and the struggle for independence. With the composition, before the nineteenth century was out, of the four *Lemminkäinen Legends*, the *Karelia* suite and, above all, *Finlandia* (1899), Sibelius seemed to embrace his role as the voice of the Finnish people.

Over the next quarter of a century, Sibelius composed his seven numbered symphonies, the violin concerto, the great tone poems — among them, *En Saga, Pohjola's Daughter, Night Ride and Sunrise* and *Tapiola* — a surprising quantity of songs with piano (few of which are at all well known outside the Nordic countries), and the incidental music to several plays, including Shakespeare's *The Tempest*. But then the music stopped. For the last thirty-one years of his life — Sibelius died in 1957 — he published nothing of any significance.

So what happened? The short answer is that we don't know. But we can make some guesses, and that means considering both his music and the reaction of audiences to his music. Sibelius's pieces were very popular in his own lifetime. Besides the secular canonisation bestowed upon him in his homeland, which in any case was partly a matter of politics and to the end was inspired by his early pieces, his music was performed widely outside Finland and Scandinavia, particularly in English-speaking countries. It is worth examining the trajectory of this fame.

In 1904, Sibelius had left the distractions (they were mostly bars) of Helsinki for a quiet life in the country. At Järvenpää, 100 kilometres north-west of the Finnish capital, he built Ainola, the house he named after his long-suffering wife Aino, and his new home soon became a magnet for visitors, a kind of shrine to the still-living composer within. In 1915, on Sibelius's fiftieth birthday, celebrated across Finland, a grand piano arrived at Ainola, a gift from a group of his admirers.

Yet for all the composer's fame, he was seldom less than impecunious. Even when he was not drinking, he came close, more than once, to financial ruin. On one of these occasions, the bailiffs came to Ainola and eyed up the precious piano. As a composer, Sibelius seems to have been driven much of the time by the need to earn money, and this resulted not so much in large-scale pieces, which after all take months if not years to produce, as in short works for piano or violin and piano — pieces that might prove popular among amateur musicians and so sell a lot of copies. Incidental music for the theatre was also an attractive proposition because it could be composed quickly to order and might result in an extended conducting engagement, supervising the pit orchestra. From 1908, he received an annual government stipend, but it was never really large enough to accommodate the composer's lifestyle, which, aside from a fondness for champagne, included the regular promotion of his own music in concerts at which he paid the orchestral players from his own pocket.

In the 1920s and 1930s, as he became more financially stable and the 'silence of Järvenpää' descended, Sibelius's fame increased. In England he was championed by conductors such as Henry Wood, Adrian Boult, John Barbirolli and especially Thomas Beecham. In the United States, Serge Koussevitzky, Leopold Stokowski and Arturo Toscanini all played his scores with great regularity. And both countries produced composers who were heavily influenced by his music. William Walton's Symphony No. 1 (1931–5) is full of the sorts of gestures one expects from Sibelius. Likewise the Symphony No. 3 of Roy Harris (1938), though its harmonies seem redolent of the American frontier, owes its temporal structure very clearly to the Finn. In 1943, Ralph Vaughan Williams's fifth symphony not only bore a dedication to Sibelius ('without permission'), but also began with gently undulating French horn calls, just as Sibelius's own fifth symphony had done.

Yet Sibelius's influence was far from universal. In 1908, as he was beginning work on his only mature string quartet (known as 'Intimate Voices'), Arnold Schoenberg, in his second string quartet, was dipping a first tentative toe into the waters of free atonality. Igor Stravinsky might have come to envy Sibelius the enormous popular success he had with *Valse triste*, but he himself composed music that was radically different rhythmically, harmonically and in nearly every other way. Béla Bartók shared Sibelius's interest in folk music, but the demotic noises he imported into his pieces and thence to the concert hall were considerably more jagged, dissonant and often plain aggressive than anything to be found in Sibelius's music. What this meant, in essence, was that while Schoenberg, Stravinsky and Bartók all presented challenges that audiences were to some extent reluctant to take up, Sibelius seemed far less of a problem to the concertgoing public. On the contrary, Sibelius's music was widely enjoyed. In 1935 when the New York Philharmonic Society polled its radio listeners, Sibelius emerged as their favourite composer, living or not. This seems extraordinary to our age. Even given the real popularity of a clutch of more-or-less minimal contemporary composers — Arvo Pärt and Philip Glass, John Tavener and Henryk Górecki (well, his third symphony anyway) — it is impossible to imagine today's classical music fans preferring the quick over the dead.

As you might imagine, Sibelius's mid-twentieth-century popularity did not especially endear him to those less popular composers who felt themselves to be more modern and so more important. After the Second World War, there began to be something like a backlash against Sibelius, not from audiences, who loved his music as much as ever, but from the musical establishment which for the next two or three decades was dominated by orthodox modernists.

The German conductor Hans Rosbaud was a champion of the modernist cause. He had worked alongside Schoenberg, Stravinsky and Bartók; in the 1950s at the Donaueschingen Festival he conducted the first performances of Olivier Messiaen's *Chronochromie*, Iannis Xenakis's *Metastasis* and György Ligeti's *Atmosphères*. Pierre Boulez's *Le Marteau sans maître*

(1955) — one of the undisputed masterpieces of the postwar avant-garde — is dedicated to Rosbaud. But the conductor's admiration for Sibelius was not something he shared with these composers or their admirers. By this point in musical history, Sibelius was viewed as an especially reactionary composer. Even another apparently reactionary composer, Benjamin Britten, complained about Sibelius's Romanticism, mentioning the Finn in the same breath as Brahms, whose music Britten loathed.

It was true, of course, that Sibelius's most recent music was now rather old, but other works from the 1920s and earlier — by Schoenberg and Webern and Stravinsky — were routinely played at new music festivals in the 1950s. In Sibelius's music what was objected to was neither its age, nor, ultimately, its popularity. After all, Debussy's *Prélude à l'après-midi d'un faune* (1894), which Boulez himself considered to mark the birth of modern music, had been so well received at its first performance that it was immediately encored. No, the postwar avant-garde composers (and festival organisers — and, in time, concert promoters and music academics) all believed that Sibelius was simply not an innovator, so they dismissed his music. They cannot have listened very hard.

Hans Rosbaud was perfectly right to champion Sibelius alongside the flag-waving modernists. For one thing, in Sibelius's music — particularly in his symphonies No. 4 (1911) and No. 5 (1915–19) — one can hear, in embryonic form, the surface textures and slow harmonic progress of late-1950s Ligeti and Xenakis. In the last movement of the fifth symphony, the superimposition of distinct rhythmic cycles moving at different speeds predicts Messiaen. In the seventh symphony (1924), which presents many movements in one, there is a structural precursor of Elliott Carter's Concerto for Orchestra (1969–70). As for Sibelius's final symphonic poem, *Tapiola* (1926), in many ways it has yet to find its later counterpart, so striking — and stark — is it in its originality. And this, surely, is the real importance of Sibelius's music. It lies not in what it might have led to, but what it actually was — and what it remains.

The trouble with most twentieth-century modernist composers was that they were somehow hoodwinked into a belief that modern music had to be atonal. Sibelius's music clearly wasn't atonal, and so they thought it couldn't be modern either. Perhaps audiences also believed it wasn't modern, and that's why they liked it so much. The theorist Theodor Adorno, who was much preoccupied with what was modern and what was not, launched a scathing critique of Sibelius, like Britten accusing him, among other things, of Romanticism.

Well Sibelius's music might not be atonal, but it isn't really tonal either. There is certainly a strong sense of harmonic gravity in his music and that comes from some especially powerful tonal centres, but the music lacks the harmonic cut and thrust of classical diatonicism, and neither does it go in for the Romantics' often wayward chromatic quests in search of a home key. Typically, Sibelius's harmony moves in slabs and moves slowly. Moreover, it might change at different rates in different strata of the music, occasionally creating the effect of gigantic grinding gears. The fifth symphony's finale is probably the most audible example of this. So this composer's use of harmony was certainly personal, and his influence is more keenly felt in a lot of present-day music than in anything composed in the intervening seventy years.

If there is one parameter of Sibelius's work that, above all the others, displays his utter originality, it is his attitude to tempo. The very fact that this was such an important issue for the composer marks him out as an individual: there is no other composer before him (though there have been plenty since) for whom the control of tempo was so vital in generating and delineating the final form of the music. One particular device that, as a composer, I continue to find inspiring, is Sibelius's ability to present many speeds under one tempo indication. At the start of Symphony No. 6 (1923), as Arnold Whittall points out in the *Cambridge Companion to Sibelius*, the apparently contradictory indication *Allegro molto moderato* ('Fast, very moderate') actually prepares us for this technique. But as early as the first movement of the Symphony No. 2 (1902), there is a bold example of the same device.

The second symphony begins with a jogging figure in the strings above which the woodwind chirp a blithe, folk-like tune in D major. Only fourteen bars into the piece, this carefree pastoral stops in its tracks, leaving behind a slowly rising horn figure that comes to rest on a foreign chord of E minor (the key of Sibelius's previous symphony). Then the woodwind tune continues (still in E minor) as though nothing had happened and returns us to D major before the horns reappear with their long slow notes to float us back up to E minor once more. All of this happens without the composer indicating any change of tempo. Unfortunately, conductors usually slow down markedly at the horns' entry. This was happening as early as 1930 when Sibelius's contemporary and friend, the conductor Robert Kajanus, recorded the symphony, but the score indicates no such slowing (that happens in the notes themselves) and the music is considerably more powerful when played straight as the composer instructs.

Sibelius's mastery of tempo is nowhere clearer than in the first movement of his Symphony No. 5. A composer's habit of revising pieces is not something that usually earns much public attention or critical praise, but often it should. Sibelius was an assiduous reviser and without exception he improved his pieces as he reworked them. When it was first performed in 1915, the fifth symphony was already very good, but by the time Sibelius had thoroughly renovated it in 1919, it had become one of his greatest pieces.

The most striking change was to the first two movements, which were now just one. The original first movement had been slow, the original second fast. Sibelius's new movement set out slowly enough and then, bit by bit, increased its speed. The last minute of the revised movement is a race, almost against time, to the double bar line. How the composer brings this off is extremely impressive and wholly individual. The tempo increases in two ways. On the one hand, there are moments when the conductor is simply told to push the tempo up a notch — but only ever one notch at a time. The other part of the process involves the multiplication of the actual notes while the tempo remains constant, so that the music appears to get faster without really doing so. Typically this happens while the harmony doesn't change at all, or changes very slowly. These techniques in combination allow the music to move from its opening *Tempo molto moderato* to its final *Presto* so gradually that one scarcely notices it happening until it is too late and the movement is hurtling to its close. There are few more thrilling climaxes in all symphonic music, and, 'modern' or not, the effect and the technique employed to achieve it were completely original.

Perhaps, after all, this is the key to Sibelius's retirement. Perhaps it was his very individualism that finally put a stop to his work. After all, most composers don't retire; many go on composing into their eighties, if they live that long. Sibelius's prolonged silence is nearly unique in the history of classical music, and one wonders whether perhaps he became artistically lonely. Not only was he composing music that was unlike anyone else's, but by the 1920s it was surely clear even to Sibelius that this was the 'wrong' sort of music. To be modern — to be relevant — one ought to be following in the footsteps of Schoenberg or Stravinsky or Bartók. Sibelius was genuinely interested in what these composers and his other contemporaries were doing, but there comes a point in any composer's life when the only thing that counts is to be yourself, and Sibelius had surely reached that point by the time of the late symphonies and *Tapiola*.

Those last decades at Järvenpää were characterised by the composer's growing international fame and his slow retreat into personal privacy. On Sibelius's important birthdays the Finnish president would make speeches, and gifts would come from around the world. On his ninetieth birthday a box of cigars arrived from Winston Churchill. That same year the Philadelphia Orchestra played in Helsinki under its chief conductor, Eugene Ormandy, another great Sibelian, and when the composer failed to appear for the concert, Ormandy hired a bus and took his players to Ainola. The frail Sibelius was brought to his front door to find an entire American symphony orchestra standing in his garden in the drizzling rain applauding him.

All this time, there was talk in musical circles across the world of an eighth symphony. To begin with, Sibelius himself spoke of it. Once he announced that the first movement was complete. On another occasion he informed the American critic Olin Downes that he had finished the whole symphony. Whatever the truth of the matter — and probably the score was fed into the stove at Ainola some time around 1940 — not a note of it was ever heard.

The expensive distractions of Maurice Ravel

The music of the dandy and dilettante Maurice Ravel enjoys the broadest appreciation accorded any concert music of the twentieth century. Other composers — from Stravinsky to Schoenberg, Rakhmaninov to Richard Strauss — might attract more ardent supporters, but they have equally ardent gainsayers. Why does everyone love Ravel?

In the years after the Second World War, music in France — and more widely in Europe — was sharply polarised into warring (actually, sneering) camps. On the one hand were those composers who felt it was time to get back to normality. The world needed cheering up, and composers such as Francis Poulenc and Jean Françaix were just the men to do it. Their pieces are full of Gallic charm and wit; this is music that inhabits a world midway between the salon and the café. But for a new generation of composers, stepping out of Messiaen's class at the Conservatoire and led by the twenty-year-old Pierre Boulez, there could be no such going back. Self-satisfaction had tacitly led to many of the century's greatest atrocities; it was time to wipe the slate clean, in music as in all else, and start again.

Ravel, who had died two years before World War II broke out, is a surprising figure to gain the admiration of both these factions. The esteem of Poulenc and Françaix is easy to explain. Was there ever a more suave composer than Ravel? His music is cool, sophisticated and synthetic. All art, he said, is illusion; it has nothing to do with real life, it is a 'divertissement de luxe' — a high-class game, an expensive distraction. And it is perfectly true: there is something artificial about his music. But there is something affectionate too. Something enchanting. Tristan Klingsor, the pseudonymous poet of Ravel's *Shéhérazade*, spoke of 'the ironic and tender heart beneath the velvet waistcoat of Maurice Ravel', and the composer himself is once supposed to have said of a mechanical bullfinch that he could feel its heart beating. All of this might have been a model for the aesthetic sensibilities of Poulenc, but it is difficult, at first, to see what Boulez admired in the work of such a debonair composer. At one point in Boulez's second piano sonata of 1947, he instructs the player to 'pulverise the sound'. One cannot imagine anything less Ravelian.

And yet not only has Boulez the conductor made some of the most accomplished modern recordings of Ravel's music — the accuracy of his ear and meticulousness of his technique being perfectly suited to the cool precision of Ravel's scores — he has also long been fascinated by the alchemy at work in the sound of Ravel's orchestra. For Boulez, Ravel is one of the most significant orchestral inventors in history, a true pioneer, adopting a research-and-development approach to his art. That art itself, however, generates further paradoxes.

Ravel was a child at heart. He learned to compose, as children learn to speak, by copying others, but this did not end when he ceased to be a student. In a century obsessed with novelty, progress and originality, Ravel liked to play 'let's pretend'. One moment he is in Spain (*Rapsodie espagnol, Alborada del gracioso, L'heure espagnol*), the next he is in Vienna (Schubert's Vienna in *Valses nobles et sentimentales*, Johann Strauss's in *La Valse*). He puts on eighteenth-century dress (*Menuet antique, Le Tombeau de Couperin*). Or he transforms himself into a gypsy (*Tzigane*), or a Greek (Five Greek Popular Songs), or an African (*Chansons madécasses*), or an African American (the 'blues' from his violin sonata).

'It is through imitation that I innovate,' Ravel once said. And it is perfectly true that, although ostensibly Viennese or Greek or eighteenth-century (or whatever), none of the above-mentioned musical works could be mistaken for the genuine article. The possible exception to this rule is the Spanish pieces but then, as Manuel de Falla once complained, the French have always composed better Spanish music than the Spanish themselves.

Ravel's own voice emerges in every bar of his music. His melodic writing, for instance, is highly distinctive, the same intervals used over and over. Once you begin spotting the falling perfect fourths in his music you will never stop. Sing the second and third notes of the Australian national anthem ('stra–lians') and you have the interval. Now get hold of a recording of Ravel's *Sonatine* for solo piano. The first two notes of the melodic line make that same descending interval: in fact the perfect fourth dominates the whole piece. The more you listen to Ravel's other music, the more you realise there are falling perfect fourths around every corner. If you add to this melodic distinction the composer's rather conventional triadic harmony, invariably spiced with 'added notes' (as in jazz), and then factor in that devastating ear for orchestral sonority, you have a very individual musical idiolect.

But although this composer is always instantly recognisable, he keeps us at arm's length. The heart might be beating, but the velvet waistcoat is tightly buttoned. With Ravel, in art as in life, appearance was important. Penetrating the appearance is nearly impossible. Looking at the many photographs of the composer, one invariably sees a man attired in the latest fashion. Leaving France for a two-month concert and lecture tour of the United States and Canada in 1928, he took along fifty-seven ties.

In addition to being classical music's snappiest dresser, Ravel was equally in thrall to artistic fashion. The adopted styles in which he worked were always *à la mode*. For example, many French artists at the beginning of the twentieth century — poets and painters as much as composers — were fascinated by Spain, just as they were by *chinoiserie* and all things oriental; in the years before the Great War, Africa was in vogue (think of the influence of African art, especially masks, on Picasso's painting); by the 1920s it was ragtime and early jazz. Ravel succumbed in turn to each of these trends, and once seduced by a particular musical type, he retained it in his inventory of styles. The opera of 1925, *L'Enfant et les sortilèges* ('The Child and the Magic Spells') is a virtual compendium of these styles. Only Spain is absent, and the composer's final work, *Don Quichotte à Dulcinée* (1932–3), complete with its dance forms the *quajira*, *zortzico* and *jota*, more than makes up for that.

Ravel was a dilettante in the best sense of the word. Often he did not even bother fully to absorb an influence; for Ravel, it was enough to like something and therefore want it in his music. The so-called 'Golden Age' of eighteenth-century French art, for instance, was one of the more profound fascinations for artists of his generation. Manuscripts were dug out of archives, scholarly editions of Rameau and Couperin were published; but what attracted Ravel was not the historical period itself, or even really the music, so much as the *idea* of the period — all those high wigs and *fêtes galantes*, harlequins and pierrots.

Le Tombeau de Couperin (1917) might adopt the outward trappings of a baroque suite, specifically the French tradition of a set of memorial pieces (*tombeau* or tomb) dedicated to a dead colleague, but five of its six movements have little direct connection to Couperin's music. The one movement that does, the *Forlane*, is actually a piece of subtle theft. Ravel made a transcription of the *Forlane* from the fourth of Couperin's

Concerts royaux, then changed a few of the notes around, before dragging it wholesale into the middle of his own piece. He did not even bother to alter the original key.

In 1913, when he composed his *Trois Poèmes de Stéphane Mallarmé*, the composer had been under the spell not only of the symbolist poet whose words he was setting, but also of Schoenberg. The Viennese composer's *Pierrot lunaire* had received its first performance in Berlin, where it impressed everyone. Word quickly spread concerning its singer/speaker, its mixed chamber ensemble, and the strange new sonorities the composer drew from both. Stravinsky was so struck by it that he dropped what he was doing (nothing important, just composing *The Rite of Spring*) to produce his *Three Japanese Lyrics* for a soprano voice and similar mixed ensemble, and Ravel wrote his *Trois Poèmes de Stéphane Mallarmé* for the same forces. The French composer even spoke of mounting a 'scandalous concert' in which *Pierrot lunaire* would be performed alongside his own and Stravinsky's work.

The Mallarmé songs are ravishing. Like *Pierrot*, they are endlessly resourceful in their use of the instrumental ensemble, and they hint strongly at a fascination with Viennese modernism and atonality; by some way, these are Ravel's most chromatic pieces. Yet even this music is the work of a dilettante. It now seems certain that Ravel had never actually heard *Pierrot lunaire* when he concocted this accomplished tribute to Schoenberg's music. Stravinsky had enthusiastically described it to him, and that was enough to send Ravel off in a new direction.

It was not only in stylistic matters that Ravel's music was, as he was the first to admit, artificial. Even Ravel's celebrated orchestral inventions were achieved in the most unlikely manner. In contrast to his contemporary and compatriot Debussy (or, for that matter, Berlioz), who from the outset imagined music in orchestral terms — hearing this phrase on an oboe, that chord on muted horns — Ravel applied his orchestration to existing music.

Ravel is famous for transforming many of his solo piano pieces into works for orchestra, and doing it so convincingly that the orchestrations completely belie their original form. But in fact every orchestral piece Ravel composed began life at the piano and was first written down as piano music. *Rapsodie espagnol*, *Daphnis et Chloé*, *La Valse*: they all started out this way. Only when Ravel was happy with the music in that state did he begin the process of transformation, applying orchestral colour to his piano originals like so many coats of paint. It is hard to believe that this was his *modus operandi* because Ravel's orchestra projects his musical ideas so naturally. But even the application of orchestral paint was unconventional. Ravel's approach to the job was to 'through-score' the music first for strings. When he was happy with what the strings were playing, when their part sounded convincing in its own right, he would begin work on the woodwind, and then later the brass. Each layer of sound was to be independently perfect. When all these small perfections were played together, Ravel reasoned, they would combine to produce one big perfection.

This is very similar to the way the *fin-de-siècle* Viennese painter Gustav Klimt worked. At Klimt's death in 1918, a half-finished canvas was discovered in his studio revealing that beneath the painter's highly ornate surfaces were other layers, equally ornate. Specifically in this work, now forever in progress, the image of a naked woman, complete and painted in minute detail, was in the process of being dressed. Before Klimt was taken to hospital, he had been hard at work covering this woman's nakedness with a golden cloak bearing his trademark decorative designs, gradually obscuring such details as individually painted pubic hairs. Knowing that Klimt worked in this way, it is hard to look at his famous paintings, such as *The Kiss*, without wondering what is beneath all that gold paint. It is, however, not just Klimt's painstaking layering of paint and images that reminds one of Ravel's working methods. There is something about the stylised poses of Klimt's figures and the gleaming golden surfaces that also suggests the Frenchman's music. Above all, perhaps, the two artists shared concerns for style and detail.

The fastidious nature of Ravel's ear led him to make dozens of small alterations when devising the orchestral versions of piano pieces. Pianists might not agree, but it is tempting to compare piano music to black-and-white photography, orchestral music to photography in colour (photographers might not agree either). With Ravel's music, we can compare colour and monochrome versions of the same 'image', and just as the contrast in a black-and-white photograph will tend to be sharper than in a colour photograph, so the individual notes in a piano chord will tend to be heard more clearly than when those same notes are given to different orchestral instruments. The softer timbres or tone colours of orchestral instruments encourage the pitches to merge, whereas the essentially percussive nature of the piano presents the notes more boldly. A good example of this is the opening bars of *Valses nobles et sentimentales*, which sound considerably more dissonant in the original solo piano guise than in the later orchestral version. The same pitches are involved, but the dissonances are sharper with the piano's sonorities.

Similarly, in the minuet of *Le Tombeau de Couperin*, gently dissonant added notes are judiciously placed to ensure that the music never seems sentimental (Ravel's music often teeters on the brink of sentimentality, but the composer goes to great pains to maintain good taste). In the orchestral suite, however, the composer's limpid orchestration weakens the effect of these dissonances and suddenly the harmonies sound dangerously sugary. The composer's solution was to increase the tempo until balance was restored and corniness banished. Pianists, then, are instructed to play the minuet at 92 beats to the minute; conductors are given the rather swifter metronome marking of 120. And if conductors would actually take the composer at his word, this piece would successfully shun sentimentality every time.

But this is a recurrent problem with Ravel's music. The composer was adamant that his pieces should be played, not interpreted. Stories of his complaints to performers are legion. After one such complaint to Toscanini, the conductor sent a telegram insisting, 'Performers shall not be slaves'. 'Performers ARE slaves,' Ravel telegrammed back.

Ravel's music is infinitely fragile. Play it too fast or too slow, distort the rhythm or ignore the dynamic markings and you risk more than unwanted sentimentality; you trivialise the music. But if you listen to the recordings made during the composer's own lifetime — especially those supervised by the composer — the music emerges with a simple freshness, devoid of interpretation and added emotion. The velvet waistcoat is firmly buttoned. The fact is that Ravel's music mirrors his personality as closely as Beethoven's or Berlioz's or Wagner's music mirrors theirs. With Ravel and with his music, one is never allowed to get too close. That is not only the music's charm, but also why it often seems so moving. One sees past — hears beyond — the restraint; one senses the beating heart of the mechanical bird.

The aphasia and apraxia that overtook Ravel in his later years only exaggerated his detachment. He withdrew further and further into himself. After the piano concertos of 1931, he found it nearly impossible to concentrate on composing. He wrote his last music in 1933. His final attempts at orchestration were dictated to an amanuensis. By 1935 he had to be shielded from autograph hunters because he could no longer write his name. Eventually, detachment overcame him; this most restrained of composers was restrained from his own music. He knew the music was still there — even as he was wheeled into the operating theatre for the brain surgery from which he would not recover, he spoke of ideas unrealised — but he could no longer reach it.

Perhaps, after all, it is the restraint that endears this composer and his music to an age that shows little restraint of its own. Perhaps we love Ravel and his music because he never harangues us, never forces our emotional response, never tells us what to think or how to feel. Instead, he offers us his expensive distractions, which are always made to the highest standard. And he keeps his distance.

Roger Nichols, in his monogram on Ravel (still perhaps the best single book on his life and work), reports a remark attributed to the composer in the latter stage of his illness. He had attended a concert at which *Daphnis et Chloé* was played. As he left, he is said to have murmured to a companion, 'Tout de même, il avait du talent, ce Ravel!' ('Even so, he had some talent, that Ravel!')

John Adams and the art of good and evil

John Adams's *El Niño* starts with a chord of D minor. It pulses away in the orchestra, gently but insistently, going nowhere, jogging on the spot. Pizzicato violins introduce a cross-rhythm, but still on the note D. This is a postmodern commonplace, a stock minimalist gesture, blank and neutral, and you think to yourself, 'Oh God, I hope it isn't going to go on like this for the whole piece'. Back in the 1960s and 1970s, you see, there were musical works that continued exactly like this for what seemed like hours on end. In *El Niño*, fortunately, it takes only about thirty seconds before other pitches are introduced and Adams's music slowly unfolds into song, a simple, ravishing setting of a Middle English lyric about the Virgin Mary, 'I sing of a maiden'.

I had listened to the recording of this modern oratorio a few times before two thoughts occurred to me in quick succession.

The first was something my friend the writer and critic Martin Buzacott had said to me many years ago. He suggested that capital-M Minimalism — the minimalism of the 1960s and 1970s, of La Monte Young and Terry Riley and Steve Reich and Philip Glass, the minimalism that used to continue the same way for hours — was only the beginning of something. Buzacott compared it to the advent of sonata form in the late eighteenth century, pointing out that the Classical style did not spring up, fully formed, in the Viennese masterpieces of Haydn, Mozart and Beethoven; there had been lesser figures before them, experimenting with the form. In particular, the Italian composer Giovanni-Battista Sammartini (c.1700–75) wrote some 2000 pieces, including probably the first-ever string quartets. Now Sammartini's vast oeuvre is not something with which we concern ourselves terribly much these days, but in there, somewhere, is the beginning of sonata form. Sammartini's experiments made possible the great music of the Classical period, and Buzacott's thesis was that Young, Riley, Reich and Glass were all Sammartinis; the really great composers of minimalism — the so-called post-minimalists — were yet to come.

The second thought that struck me, listening to those first bars of *El Niño*, was that there is a precedent for starting a large-scale oratorio with this sort of empty neutrality. At the beginning of *The Creation*, Haydn depicts the chaos of the cosmos not as a baroque composer might have done, with a dense, weird, chromatic chord, but with a single pitch. This one note represents the void better than any chord could, however weird. A chord, which is an aggregation of pitches, is a very specific piece of information. There are only so many possible outcomes for this information, only so many ways of following any particular chord (at least, if you are a Classical composer). But one note? This tells you nothing. There is no information to build on, nothing to follow. You listen to this single, lonely pitch and you cannot predict a thing about the way the music will progress. Anything might happen next. Or nothing. This is authentic chaos.

Well, that is just how you feel at the start of *El Niño*. You are waiting to see in which direction the music will move, hoping that it will move somewhere, afraid that it may not. Even the pulsing rhythm and the rippling texture give you no clues, because you've heard them so many times before — in Riley, in Glass, in the music of those twentieth-century Sammartinis. And when Adams's music does move away from this opening sound in *El Niño*, it is as though the composer is waving it goodbye.

If Buzacott is right, then, and if my imagination isn't acting up, John Adams must be the Haydn for our times. It is a big claim certainly, but since the early 1990s Adams's music has flowered in a particularly rich and complex fashion that could no more have been envisaged by Terry Riley composing his radical repetitions in the mid-1960s than poor old Sammartini could have imagined Haydn's 'London' symphonies. Anyway, Adams ought to be used to hype by now. He has had a lot of it.

Ever since the impact of his opera *Nixon in China* (1987) began to sink in, John Adams has been, for some, America's greatest composer. For others, he has been the world's greatest composer (Howard Goodall, I think, described him thus in his television series *Big Bangs*). At a retrospective of Adams's music in London in 2002, he was called 'The Voice of America'. Perhaps he was riding for a fall. On 9 December 2001 in the *New York Times*, he became John Adams, romancer of terrorists, whose 1991 opera *The Death of Klinghoffer* might be read as 'anti-American, anti-Semitic and anti-bourgeois'.

These are the words of one of classical music's most respected analysts and commentators, Richard Taruskin. From his base at the Berkeley campus of the University of California, Taruskin has produced some of the best modern writing about music. On Musorgsky and Shostakovich, he has written with originality and illumination, and in 1997 he produced the two-volume, 1757-page *Stravinsky and the Russian Traditions* which said so many new things about the twentieth century's most famous composer and his music that one hardly believed it possible the information had not been available before. In 2005, he published the six-volume, 4272-page *Oxford History of Western Music*, not as its editor, but as its writer — of every word. So Taruskin's opinions are listened to and applauded. If he says your opera is anti-American or anti-Semitic, he tends to be believed.

In late 2001, Taruskin suffered what looked very much like a critical meltdown. It came in the wake of the terrorist attacks on New York and Washington, and the first evidence I saw of it was at the end of November in the letters page of the *London Review of Books*. Following that journal's decision to invite its regular contributors to comment on the events of September 11, and in particular following the publication of comments in the 'America had it coming' vein, Taruskin wrote to the magazine announcing that he was taking his ball home. He had finished his promised Shostakovich review, he told the editors and readers, but they would never see it! Shortly after came his piece about John Adams in the *New York Times*.

The Death of Klinghoffer, Adams's second opera, concerns the hijacking of the Italian cruise ship *Achille Lauro*, and the murder by Arab terrorists of the Jewish passenger Leon Klinghoffer. As chance would have it, it was first performed in Brussels in March 1991 at the height of the first Gulf War, when it was received enthusiastically enough, if not with quite the same ecstasy that had greeted *Nixon*. However, at its American premiere in Brooklyn later that year, there was controversy, fuelled by Klinghoffer's real-life daughters calling the opera anti-Semitic. Adams says that this was presumably because it didn't offer 'a blanket condemnation of the Palestinian cause'.

In the years since its premiere, the opera has not fared especially well. True, it was quickly released on CD, which is more than happens to 99.9 per cent of new operas, but for the next decade the work had few live outings. That changed at the start of the twenty-first century, with performances in Helsinki, London and Amsterdam and an impressive filmed account of the work directed by Penny Woolcock. But an attempt to perform sections of *Klinghoffer* in the United States shortly after 11 September 2001 was cancelled. The Boston Symphony Orchestra, which was to have given the concert performance, decided to 'err on the side of being sensitive'. The composer claimed this was censorship, and that, in turn, prompted Taruskin's *New York Times* article.

Taruskin's line was that he was completely opposed to censorship, which 'is always deplorable', but he believed the Boston Symphony Orchestra was right to cancel the performances since this was no more than 'the exercise of forbearance', which, in contrast to censorship, 'can be noble'. It is certainly an interesting quiddity. Perhaps Taruskin's judgment was clouded by the anger he obviously felt (and most people shared) at the attacks on the United States, but his article was by no means just a moral muddle. He made some interesting points about the power of art, and while I suspect John Adams might have found it hard to agree with the critic's line, I am not so sure about Adams's long-time collaborator, the stage director Peter Sellars.

It was Sellars who 'masterminded' (Taruskin's rather loaded word) *The Death of Klinghoffer*. Adams might have composed the music and Alice Goodman the libretto, but Sellars was the catalyst for the opera, just as he had been for *Nixon in China*, and he directed both premieres. He was also responsible for helping to shape the libretto of *El Niño*, for directing the accompanying film and for staging the work's premiere in Paris.

Peter Sellars is a complex, sometimes confusing and (as the 2002 Adelaide Festival board discovered too late) occasionally exasperating artist, but he has always been, above all, a political artist. His work acknowledges that our individual experiences of life depend, at least partly, on how powerful we are. Power — who has it, how they use it and to what ends — determines the social structure in which each of us lives. In his stage work at the end of the twentieth century, Sellars dealt more and more explicitly with the suffering experienced by the powerless. For example, his staging in Europe and America of Bach's Cantata No. 82, *Ich habe genug* ('I have enough'), opened with the mezzosoprano soloist dressed in a white hospital gown and grey bedsocks, plastic tubing coming from her body, lying on the floor of a bare stage. The sung texts of *El Niño* and the film that accompanies the piece also testify to Sellars's concern with injustice.

El Niño is a Nativity Oratorio, and at one level — the surface level — it is about the birth of Jesus Christ. Its model, from the storytelling point of view, might be Berlioz's *L'Enfance du Christ*; in terms of its structure and its use of different texts and different angles, the model, as Adams readily acknowledges, is Handel's *Messiah*. And yet *El Niño* is in no obvious or traditional sense a religious work; it tells its story of a miraculous birth with texts from the Bible, including the New Testament Apocrypha, together with other sources. It is the extra-biblical dimension, one imagines, for which Sellars is largely responsible. For the most part, these other sources are Latin American, the words of four poets being heard alongside the biblical verses, telling of pregnancy, childbirth, motherhood and loss. We hear of the joy of conception and the pain of childbirth. Herod's massacre of the innocents is juxtaposed with a long poem about the massacre of perhaps 300 students in Mexico City's Tlatelolco Square in 1968. Meanwhile, on the screen, a parallel story is played out by Latin American actors, the miraculous birth taking place in a car park.

You might argue that this updating of the Christmas story is scarcely more radical than the sort of thing that might be attempted by a primary-school teacher with dramatic ambitions: since stables are a foreign concept to most modern city-dwelling children, a car park will do very nicely. But Sellars, one suspects, has a wider social agenda.

'Peter believes that art really has a kind of moral power that can bring about social change,' Adams said in an interview. Adams himself, significantly, has doubts about this notion, believing that any moral power that art might have is at best 'spiritual'. When he points out that Beethoven's ninth symphony saved no lives, he echoes W. H. Auden's remark that poetry makes nothing happen. Anyway, Adams says, he does not like preaching.

Considering their collaborations on *Nixon*, *Klinghoffer* and *El Niño*, it would be simplistic to imagine an apolitical Adams merely providing the soundtrack to staged agitprop 'masterminded' by Sellars. Adams was interested in American history and politics long before Peter Sellars came along. In the early 1970s, when Sellars was still in high school, Adams was composing pieces that held up a mirror to the mores of contemporary America — of Richard Nixon's America. In a triptych of pieces collectively entitled *American Standard* (1973) Adams included a panel called *Christian Zeal and Activity*. In the only commercially available recording, a Southern Baptist preacher is enthusiastically retelling the story of Christ healing a withered arm. Against this, a hymn tune is played, the voices that make up the usual block chords floating free in what the composer calls 'dream polyphony'. In an earlier version of the piece, recorded for an LP on Brian Eno's Obscure Music label, the floating hymn was the same, but instead of the preacher's voice one heard a slice of late-night talkback evangelical radio. In neither version of the piece, however, did Adams tell us what to think. When he says today, 'I don't like preaching', he may or may not be talking about the kind of preaching heard in *Christian Zeal and Activity*; he is certainly talking about art that sets out to change the world.

In *On the Transmigration of Souls*, the piece Adams composed in 2002 to commemorate those who died in the attacks on New York and Washington, the tone is, for the most part, deliberately neutral. The piece opens and closes with ambient sounds recorded in New York City. The names of the dead are read out. We might be hearing a musical equivalent of the Vietnam War Memorial in Washington — a simple and very beautiful wall of polished granite bearing the names of the soldiers killed in the conflict. Nobody needed a musical 9/11 memorial that told them what to think. People knew what to think. *On the Transmigration of Souls* leaves them the space to go on thinking.

The Death of Klinghoffer, it seems to me, is a rather similar work. I hear no sides being taken in this opera, only an even-handed treatment of the Israeli–Palestinian situation. I fear it was this very evenhandedness that raised hackles in the United States after 11 September 2001. Doubtless Taruskin would consider me naive or, worse, disingenuous. But when he accused Adams of turning the *Achille Lauro* terrorists into glamorous Robin Hoods, he seemed to me to have abandoned perspective. And when he insisted, in his article, that the only way to defeat terrorism was 'to focus resolutely on the acts rather than their claimed (or conjectured) motivations, and to characterize all such acts, whatever their motivation, as crimes', I suspect he was pushing a political barrow of his own.

And this is what was particularly interesting in the shemozzle between Adams and Sellars and Taruskin: of the three, it was Adams who was the odd man out.

'In the wake of September 11,' Taruskin wrote, 'we might want, finally, to get beyond sentimental complacency about art. Art is not blameless. Art can inflict harm. The Taliban know that [in Afghanistan the Taliban had recently been blowing the faces off giant stone-carved Buddhas]. It's about time we learned.'

I think Peter Sellars would agree with this. If art can be a force for good, it follows that it must also be possible for it to 'inflict harm'. Naturally, Sellars would not agree that *The Death of Klinghoffer* does this, but I am guessing that he and Taruskin would mostly argue over examples.

As for John Adams, he might be a man who believes in causes, but he is primarily an instinctive artist who believes even more, I think, in the 'pure good' of art — with the emphasis on 'pure'.

At the end of *El Niño*, the orchestra fades away, the other voices drop out, and a children's choir is left singing (in Spanish) these words by Rosario Castellanos, to the gently rocking accompaniment of an acoustic guitar:

From the dark land of men
I've come kneeling to behold you.
Tall, naked, alone.
A poem.

There is nothing about politics here, you notice. Nothing about making the world a better place or all men being brothers. But then Adams is our Haydn, not our Beethoven.

Kaija Saariaho and the sound of music

At the beginning of Kaija Saariaho's piece for alto flute, cello and orchestra, ... *à la fumée*, you might be forgiven for imagining a wintry light shining through a forest of birch trees heavy with snow, particularly if you know the composer's nationality. The music, composed in 1990, is typical of Saariaho's work of that time, which seemed to specialise in high-pitched flutes and strings, glittering percussion sonorities, slow tempos and static harmonies. It does not take much imagination to hear this music in the context of the glacial landscapes that are Sibelius's fourth symphony, *Night Ride with Sunrise*, *Tapiola* and *Scene with Cranes* And there is possibly some truth in it too.

But apart from the fact that it must be galling for every Finnish composer automatically to be measured against

Sibelius, it would also be misleading to explain Saariaho's music only in terms of her nationality. For one thing, Saariaho, who turned fifty in 2002, is very much an international figure, her music commissioned and performed by orchestras throughout Europe and the United States. She is also a long-time expatriate. She has lived in Paris since the early 1980s, her music sharing a very French concern with the quality of sound.

All music is sound. Even when musicians are looking at music on the page they are turning it into sound in their heads. And so it seems surprising that very little Western music has proceeded from an exploration of the nature of sound. In fact, in the work of most of the great composers of classical music, sound itself has tended to be taken for granted.

The major exception to this rule, as with many other rules, was Hector Berlioz. In the scene at the Capulets' tomb from the dramatic symphony *Roméo et Juliette*, the musical fabric is suddenly fractured and we are left listening to a solo clarinet. It is playing isolated pitches that might once have added up to a melodic line, but no longer do. What is most expressive here is the sonority of the instrument. The clarinet is in the part of its range where it produces its weakest tone, and when he asked for this, Berlioz, an expert in these matters, knew exactly what he was doing. The instrument sounds vulnerable; its occasional crescendos are strained and pathetic. At this moment in the piece, Berlioz is more concerned with the sound of the instrument than with the notes it is playing. A more extreme and more famous example occurs in *Symphonie fantastique*. At the end of the third movement, the timpani players execute simultaneous long rolls on two, then three, then finally four kettledrums. Berlioz even specified the sponge-headed sticks with which they should do it. It is the first instance of drum chords in Western music, and it is undertaken in the spirit of an acoustic experiment.

In the twentieth century, when modernist artists were asking some particularly hard questions of themselves regarding both the style of their work and, just as urgently, the point of it all, composers inevitably poked and prodded at the very materials of their music. They explored the quality of sound, not only in terms of applying orchestration to abstract musical ideas or even composing directly on to specific instruments, but also by extracting music from sonority itself. The colours or *timbres* of sounds were more than the clothing in which the music was dressed up; they could also be the music. In particular, in the later twentieth century, composers such as the Romanian-born Greek Iannis Xenakis and the Hungarian György Ligeti produced works that were vast, slow-moving clouds of orchestral sonority.

Romanian Horatiu Radulescu created sometimes cloud-like musical structures derived from the purest sounds of all, the natural harmonics of vibrating objects. Concentrating on the higher overtones of the harmonic series, Radulescu invented 'spectral' harmony, steering his music away from the equal-tempered scale that had dominated music since Bach's day. Following Radulescu's emigration to France in 1969, a generation of French composers fell under his spell and it was among these composers, including figures such as Tristan Murail and Gérard Grisey, that Kaija Saariaho found herself on her arrival in Paris.

Saariaho was in her element. In Finland, together with Magnus Lindberg and Esa-Pekka Salonen, she had been part of the group of young composers known as *Korvat auki* ('Ears Open'); now she was having her own ears opened. What Saariaho found among the French spectralists, however, was rather more than a new attitude to harmony. Like Ligeti before her — indeed, like Berlioz — Saariaho was at least as interested in the timbral possibilities of the instruments and their overtones.

At IRCAM, Pierre Boulez's institute for musical and acoustic research attached to the Georges Pompidou Centre, Saariaho used the latest computer technology to analyse instrumental timbres. In particular, she was interested in the gamut of timbres from the purest possible to the noisiest. Flute tones were recorded, ranging from a pitch with the minimum of breath through to breath alone; a cellist was asked to apply increasing amounts of bow pressure from the lightest to the heaviest, until you could hear little but the noise of the bow on the string. From the information she gathered, Saariaho composed a series of works for instruments and electronics. Not only do the sonic data themselves feature in her electronic music, but also, like the spectralists, she derived her harmonic language from these investigations and then, by extension, she went on to educe most of the other formal properties of her music from the same source.

It sounds impossibly technical, but the result was some of the most ravishing music of the 1980s. In *Lichtbogen* ('Arc of Light'), the piece that in 1985 really launched her career outside Finland, Saariaho attempted a musical depiction of the Northern Lights. The instrumental and electronic sounds are predominantly high in pitch (flute tones and cello harmonics to the fore) and they shift very slowly. The debt to orchestral music of the 1960s, especially that of Ligeti, is apparent in the way Saariaho exploits texture as much as harmony for her music's expression and development. Ligeti himself had moved on to something quite different by 1985, but it was Saariaho's considerable achievement to demonstrate that there was much mileage still in sound for sound's sake.

The change of direction in Ligeti's music, at the time seeming more like a derailment, was brought on by his opera *Le Grand Macabre* (1977). Operas have a habit of making composers change: they force their creators to deal with drama and stage time, which are not necessarily the same as musical time or even compatible with it, and they insist upon the audibility of words. While it is perfectly true that singers have frequently failed to deliver clear diction, hence the modern predilection for surtitles even for operas in the language of the audience, the *attempt* to make words comprehensible is often a salutary lesson for a composer. And then there is the singing itself. Sooner or later, the human voice seems to demand lyricism.

All this appears to have struck Ligeti with great force. By the time Saariaho composed *Lichtbogen*, Ligeti, his opera behind him, had emerged as a composer of clearly recognisable melodies. Off in the distance, a similar derailment awaited Saariaho, though one suspects she saw it coming and so made her approach with care.

As with Ligeti, Saariaho's change of style came about thanks to an opera. In 2000, *L'amour de loin* ('Love from Afar') received its world premiere at the Salzburg Festival, which had commissioned it. The stage direction was by Peter Sellars, showing uncharacteristic restraint, and the piece was well received by those who attended.

L'amour de loin has a libretto by the Lebanese-born French-based writer Amin Maalouf. It concerns the life of the twelfth-century troubadour Jaufré Rudel, Prince of Blaye, and his ideal of love for Clémence, the Countess of Tripoli, a woman he has never met. In these days of Internet relationships I suppose there is something curiously modern about the story itself, but Saariaho's attraction to the tale seems to have been at least partly concerned with the aesthetics of Europe in the Middle Ages. As early as 1993, in an electro-acoustic piece inspired by the mediaeval tapestry of the Lady and the Unicorn, Saariaho had begun exploring the subject of courtly love that would lead to this opera. And in that work, which employs both a singing voice as well as a speaking voice, the lyricism of her music seems quite suddenly to have flowered.

Vocal music came to dominate this composer's work during the 1990s, the opera being the culmination of that process. *Lonh*, for soprano and electronics, was a kind of sketch for the major work. It sets a text by Jaufré Rudel in the Provençal language (*Lonh* means 'Afar' — 'loin' in modern French). The piece, which is one of Saariaho's loveliest, was later incorporated wholesale into the opera.

Among Saariaho's more recent works, even those that are not vocal seem to sing. The flute concerto *Aile du songe* (literally, 'Wing of the dream') begins and ends with sonic rustlings, the evocative timbres so characteristic of the composer's earlier instrumental writing, but these sounds only frame a singing lyricism from the soloist, which in turn gives way to ecstatic dance rhythms.

There remains something rather detached about all Kaija Saariaho's music, but with each new piece it seems to be gaining in warmth. And so, to return to the initial conundrum as this composer bathes increasingly in the soft golden glow of twelfth-century Provence and the lyricism it has inspired, what of the wintry light of Finland? And what about Sibelius?

The frozen sounds of *Lichtbogen* and ... *à la fumée* might have been behind her by the beginning of the twenty-first century, but in embracing song Saariaho was being stereotypically Finnish. Sibelius is best known to the world at large as a composer of orchestral music, of symphonies and tone poems, but he wrote well over a hundred songs, and in the country of his birth some of these are as popular as *Finlandia* and the violin concerto. Until the Finnish language began to be written down (as late as the sixteenth century), singing was one of the best ways of keeping it alive. Even today, singing is an everyday activity for a lot of Finns, about 20 per cent of whom sing in choirs, while Finland has a proud tradition of supplying opera singers to the world's stages. One of the biggest contemporary names in opera, Karita Mattila, became the dedicatee of Saariaho's song cycle *Quatre instants* (2003), settings of more texts by Maalouf, who by now was the composer's regular collaborator. Again the subject was love, and the music was ever more lyrical.

Far from abandoning her roots, then, it seemed Kaija Saariaho was rediscovering them in song. And a continued vocal presence in her work was having a striking effect on the nature of her music. Where once timbre had dictated the shape of her pieces, now it was melody. As intervals widened and lines lengthened, the contours of her melodic writing grew ever more undulating; simultaneously, Saariaho's harmonies became richer and darker. The very sound of her music — still as important as ever — had blossomed. A long Finnish winter had apparently turned to spring.

Things fall apart in the music of Ross Bolleter

You know that old upright piano in your garage? The one your grandmother bought for your father to learn on, that your own children had their lessons on, the one their teacher suggested you trade in for a better model? The one that's not been tuned since 1974 and has been out in the garage since 1989 and got wet the year after when the roof leaked; that you heard the scratching from and subsequently found mice nesting in, and that you'd get someone to take away only it's ridiculously expensive; or you'd take to the tip yourself except, if you moved it, it would probably fall apart and injure you? Well, there is a man in Western Australia who would rather play your piano than a brand-new Steinway grand. His name is Ross Bolleter and he is one of Australia's most interesting and distinctive composers.

Bolleter was born in 1946, but there is something about him that is forever young. It comes out in a puckish enthusiasm for his work, an ability to lace the undoubtedly serious nature of his music with humour, identifying the absurdities of life and laughing at them. In this, I suppose, he resembles John Cage except that where Cage's laughter was wheezy and long-drawn-out, Bolleter's staccato guffaws bellow loudly and they come and go without warning.

As a composer, Bolleter has spent the majority of his career away from the concert hall. He has composed for radio, film and television, and he supplements this income by working as a cabaret pianist and accordionist. But there is an altogether less commercial side to Bolleter that involves pianos and accordions. And not just any old pianos and accordions.

I think it was André Previn who I heard tell the story of turning up to play at a small music club in the USA. Before the concert, he made his way to the stage only to discover that the piano, while technically still playable, was badly in need of an overhaul. Jokingly he suggested to the promoter that the last person to play the instrument must have been Dave Brubeck, the jazz pianist famous for his hammering style. The promoter looked amazed and told Previn he was right, Brubeck had indeed been there only the previous week. I might have forgotten one or two details of the story, but that is the gist, and the point of it is that the piano is a delicate instrument, its precision mechanism requiring regular attention from a highly trained technician. You should never, for example, leave your piano out on a tennis court during an oppressively hot West Australian summer. At least, not unless you want Ross Bolleter to show up on your property.

By the time Bolleter arrived at Nallan sheep station, in the Murchison goldfields area of Western Australia, some 700 kilometres north-east of Perth, the piano had been brought in from the tennis court. It was wintering in the tractor shed and this is where the composer first made its acquaintance. For Bolleter, it was love at first sight.

Bolleter makes the subtle distinction between pianos that are ruined and those that are either merely neglected or completely devastated. For example, a ruined piano, according to the composer, 'has its frame and bodywork more or less intact (even though the soundboard is cracked wide open, with the blue sky shining through) so that it can be played in the ordinary way'. In contrast, devastated pianos are generally so far gone that one must crouch or even lie down beside them in order to play them.

Following its abandonment to all weathers on the tennis court, the Nallan piano was ruined but not devastated. Back in the 1930s John Cage came up with the notion of a prepared piano, in which screws and bolts and rubber erasers were inserted between the piano strings in order to effect a wholesale change of the instrument's timbre. Instead of sounding like a piano tuned to an even-tempered scale, it took on the quality of a box of toy percussion instruments, tuned to some private and unpredictable system of its own. Bolleter's ruined pianos often sound like this, too, but instead of being prepared to a composer's specifications, they have been prepared by history and by geography. Time has taken its toll of these instruments, but the more pronounced changes were wrought by the environment in which they were abandoned. These pianos were prepared by the landscape; they were prepared by the weather; conceivably, the local fauna have also prepared them. And they sound magnificent.

In the Nallan tractor shed, Ross Bolleter approached the 1920s Jackson piano. As he lifted the rotten keyboard lid, it came away in his hands. He strung his microphones over a beam and set about extracting the music that remained in the piano, plucking the strings and tapping the keys. Not only music, but also armies of ants emerged from the instrument as it clattered and growled and pinged.

And now those same sounds are coming from my CD player. The clatters emanate from both the keyboard and the pedals and it is primarily through their percussive sonorities that we sense the instrument's struggle to communicate. The growls, growing to roars, come from the lower strings, silent for too long and anxious to be heard. The pings, from higher up, seem more reticent. At first, all these noises are strange, strained. It is almost painful to hear them. But with time and a little patience one enters the piano's world. The environment around the piano — the tractor shed and the world outside it — starts to recede. The distant conversation of April and Dave Petersen, owners of the sheep station, and their daughter Emmy, the yet more distant voices of birds and dogs, gradually disappear and one is caught up, more and more, in Bolleter's developing relationship with the Jackson.

'After a time,' Bolleter writes, 'I knew that April wanted to talk, was about to talk. I pointed frantically up to the Nanyo and Sanyo microphones with my right hand while trying to finish the piece with my left. Finally, she broke in — "Have you finished?" And I had.'

And that is how it finishes on the CD: with April Petersen's question. I don't know whether to think of this music as an improvisation or a composition, and I don't suppose it really matters, the main difference between the two being the degree of spontaneity involved. Back in the tractor shed, it was improvisation. But now, coming out of the loudspeakers of my stereo, the music seems composed. Moreover — and I know this will sound very strange — it seems to have been composed by the piano itself.

Bolleter has called the piece *Unfinished Business*. It is an appropriate title for the excavation of these last sounds lingering in the wreckage of what was once, presumably, the pride of its owners. And indeed this piano originally had plenty of business, entertaining the patrons of the Big Bell Hotel in the 1930s and 1940s. One pictures it as the centre of attention, the Saturday night drinkers gathered around, their voices raised in a communal rendition of 'Roll out the Barrel'. Or whatever. But as Ed Baxter, writing in *The Wire*, has observed, 'the beautiful crashes, trembles and shudders' that make up the piano's current repertoire are 'the dissolution of contemporary domesticity, summoning up visions of a wilderness only fitfully kept at bay by the partition walls'. The wood and minerals from which the piano was forged are slowly returning to their natural state.

One might go further and hear these sounds as the sonic representation of what happens to European culture when it is transplanted in Australian soil. It takes time, but the soil wins.

Whenever I am pressed, really pressed, by people outside Australia (and sometimes even in Australia) to say what Australian music sounds like, I will, of course, mention Peter Sculthorpe, and pieces such as *Mangrove* and *Earth Cry*. I will also mention David Lumsdaine's *Kelly Ground* and *Mandala 5* and his environmental compositions such as *Pied Butcherbirds of Spirey Creek*. But I usually end up plumping for Ross Bolleter's ruined pianos. As with Sculthorpe's music, there is sometimes an explicit connection with the landscape of the country. And as with Lumsdaine's pieces, birdsong is never far away. But in Bolleter's music for ruined pianos the country is literally present. It is not simply a matter of these instruments, these ambassadors of European culture, having lost something with their exposure to the passing years and the aggressive Australian climate. They have also gained something. One culture has been replaced by another.

'All that fine nineteenth-century European craftsmanship,' Bolleter writes of a degrading pianola, 'all the damp and unrequited loves of Schumann, Brahms and Chopin dry out and degrade into a heap of rotten wood and rusting wire. The pianola's dusky melodies become the harsh and common parlance of dogs, crows and sheep station owners complaining about the drought.'

Bolleter is not only a composer, he is also a storyteller. His pianos have histories and so do his accordions — he composes for asthmatic accordions with perforated bellows — and very often his music has an extra layer, the composer himself speaking to us. It might be about anything — his impressions of the environment in which the ruined instrument was discovered, his memories of David Helfgott, the time his house was robbed and the things that were stolen. My own favourites among Bolleter's stories are the 'accordion lives' which he recounts on his CD *The Night Moves on Little Feet*. We learn of the former lives of the somewhat decrepit instruments he is playing; we hear about their former owners and how they came to Australia with their instruments.

'What grabs my imagination,' Bolleter says, 'are conceptual pieces where ordinary life is intruding everywhere. Most of my impulse to work in traditional forms is absorbed in composing for film and video where the possibilities for humour and subversion lie so close to hand (and one can reach for a sardonic waltz, fugue or tango …). I continue to be strongly attached to working collaboratively with visual and conceptual artists, poets, philosophers and animals.'

Bolleter's art is inclusive; it admits the whole world. Even when it is at its most intimate (and there is no other word for some of his ruined piano pieces), he is inviting. And indeed sometimes he invites the whole world, as when, for instance, he leads a simultaneous improvisation by left-handed pianists in radio studios in Fremantle, Colorado Springs and Samarin, Slovakia (*The Left Hand of the Universe*).

For Ross Bolleter, as for the sandpiper in Elizabeth Bishop's poem, 'The world is a mist. And then the world is / minute and vast and clear.' One minute, he is attending to the smallest details of sound. The next, he is sending them around the world. And the more parochial these details, the more universal they seem. Most of Bolleter's music begins from something local and personal. For example, writing to me in an email, Bolleter mentions the LP recording he had as a teenager of Schnabel playing the Beethoven Opp. 101 and 109 'at tempos so unbelievably fast that unsuspected countries emerged, and notes fell off everywhere, the ancient recording so plangy and plangent and hissy, you could reasonably talk of a ruined recording, if not a ruined performance'. Bolleter locked himself in his room, as teenagers will, and listened to these two works over and over.

'In some sense they saved my life, shaped it,' he says, 'and when I listen to, for instance [Bolleter's ruined piano piece] *Nallan Void*, I can sense the impress of those works performed in that way by just those means.'

The more the pieces are about Bolleter, the more they appear to be about us. Bolleter's music for ruined pianos speaks with such a directly emotional voice because it taps into our collective childhood. I suspect that most of us have our first (and in most cases, our last) experience of *real* music — that is to say, music played and composed by ourselves — on a piano in a state of some disrepair. My own first composition was created and performed on the piano in my grandmother's front parlour. The piano was not ruined, but it was certainly neglected, and the composition that issued forth from 'the boom of the tingling strings' (D. H. Lawrence this time) was called 'The Animals in the Jungle'. I was maybe five. My parents and grandparents listened with stoic indulgence.

I have no idea what became of that piano, but now, as I listen to Bolleter's instruments, it is not just the heat of a West Australian summer I sense, not just the dogs and the crows and the station owners. I am also transported to the front parlour of my grandparents' house in Kirkdale, Liverpool. It is cold and dank, because it is never used. My grandparents always sit in the back of their house, reserving the parlour for who knows what: a royal visit, perhaps. I can feel the cold and I can smell the thick twist in my grandfather's pipe and, just, through the cloud of aromatic smoke, my grandmother's rice pudding baking in the oven.

My grandparents are long dead, their house pulled down, and the piano probably ended its days being smashed to pieces with sledgehammers at a fairground. But Bolleter's music brings it all back. You see, like all the best art, Ross Bolleter's music not only takes us into its own world, it also takes us deep into ourselves.

PART THREE

Making Notes

The Waltz Book (1998-2002)

There is a scene in the 1938 Hollywood movie *The Great Waltz*, in which Johann Strauss and a soprano with one of those trilling Snow White voices ride through a vividly painted cardboard replica of the Vienna Woods. Miraculously, the horse pulling their carriage trots in triple time, and the combined rhythm of the wheels and the horse's hooves quickly inspires a waltz from the composer. A passing post-horn contributes a phrase; the carriage driver's gee-up calls supply another. It's all that poor Strauss can do to keep up with the torrent of musical ideas as 'Tales from the Vienna Woods' presents itself to him, fully orchestrated, in little over a minute.

Between April 1998 and September 2002 I composed sixty waltzes and on none of them did I receive assistance from a post-horn or a horse, although eventually I accepted inspiration from anywhere I could get it. The question I have most been asked since embarking on the project is where this hitherto unsuspected fascination with the waltz came from. The answer used to be that I had no fascination with the waltz whatsoever; but slowly and inexorably, over the four and a half years I spent with this project, a kind of fascination — sometimes resembling a dogged obsession — did begin to grow.

I should explain that the term 'waltz' needs to be understood in the sense of a concert piece, an abstraction of the dance form. There has been a tradition of such pieces — and even sets of pieces — as long as the history of the waltz itself. Beethoven's hour-long *Diabelli* Variations is based on a waltz. Schubert and Brahms wrote sets of waltzes and so did Chopin. Liszt wrote them; Ravel wrote *Valses nobles et sentimentales*, inspired by Schubert. Most of these piano waltzes can't really be danced to; this is music for the fingers not the toes. The problem, very largely, is one of unsteadiness of tempo. To take someone sweeping around a ballroom with any degree of confidence, you must be able to rely on the tempo's consistency; you need to know that when you put your foot down, there will be a strong beat to accompany it. An abrupt *ritardando* (a slowing of tempo) or a delayed cadence, however musically elegant, would be apt to make the dancers fall over. Of course it is just such stylish equivocations — a hesitation, a shrug, a raised eyebrow — that typify the concert waltz. And in composing my waltzes, I was the one who nearly fell over.

The genesis of *The Waltz Book* was this. In November 1997, I received a phone call from the pianist Ian Munro, inviting me to write him a new solo work. 'Something big,' he said. 'Like a sonata.' It had been some little while since I had composed for solo piano and I greatly admired Ian's playing. So, flattered and delighted to have been asked, I said yes. Over the next few weeks, I occasionally considered the request and I began to wonder whether it might be possible to construct 'something big' out of lots of 'something small'. It would be a mosaic. The little musical tiles would be individual entities, but they would also add up to a large-scale statement. A minute seemed like the obvious length for each component, but in addition to having the same dimensions, the tiles of my mosaic seemed to call for a further unifying feature. Since the concept of the minute-waltz already existed, it occurred to me that this might provide it. I would compose seventeen minute-waltzes, adding up to a single seventeen-minute piece. (Don't ask me why seventeen.)

The next time I saw Ian Munro, I put it to him. I have forgotten now his exact words, but I remember the look on his face. He was trying hard to retain his composure, but it was plain that he thought the idea was pretty stupid. A few weeks later, however, I saw him again. Over a bottle or two of wine, he told me he had been giving some thought to my suggestion and he was coming around to it.

'But what if you were to write sixty of them?' he said. 'An hour's worth.' As the evening panned out, this began to seem like an entirely sensible notion. It would be a flexible work, and so, endlessly useful. A pianist might choose from among the waltzes, playing them individually, or as a group. Then, if time and ambition permitted, it would always be possible to present the entire hour-long kit and caboodle. We toasted Ian's idea.

A grant application was submitted to the Australia Council and, to see what it felt like, I wrote a minute-waltz. One of my radio producers had just had a baby boy, and so I called the piece 'Waltz for Jasper'. It felt good to be working in miniature, fashioning a piece that had a beginning, a middle and an end — and even a climax of sorts — but which lasted just sixty seconds; a piece in which every note, every dynamic marking counted. By the time Ian learned, some six months later, that his funding application had been successful, I had written two more waltzes. I suppose it should have been obvious to me at this point that a strike rate of three waltzes every six months was not going to see the piece completed quickly. Certainly, this was about as far as it was possible to get from the celluloid Strauss's experience in the Vienna Woods. His waltz had taken him a minute to compose; each of mine might have occupied a minute in performance, but it seemed they were taking an average of two months to write. Still, I reasoned, these initial waltzes were produced before confirmation that the big piece would actually go ahead. Surely such a slow strike rate could not be considered typical. But it *was* typical. By the time *The Waltz Book* was complete, little Jasper was virtually dating.

Perhaps it was the discipline of the minute; perhaps it was the necessity of triple time; perhaps it was simply the daunting fact that there were fifty-seven of them still to compose. Whatever the reason, writing these waltzes was like getting blood from a stone. Each time I finished one, I would tot up my progress so far. I always seemed to have more than fifty of them left. Eventually it occurred to me that I was composing these pieces with no proper rationale (besides earning my fee). Later — three years later — when the first pieces of the mosaic were finally assembled and I could see where the gaps were, I knew that a fast waltz was required here, a loud waltz there, a simple waltz over there with a rather spiky, dissonant one just beside it. But right now I was producing minute-waltzes more or less at whim, and all I had to stimulate my imagination was the length and the triple metre. It was clear I required a plan.

The first and most obvious plan, building on that waltz marking Jasper's arrival in the world, was to derive 'inspiration' from other dedications. As it gradually expanded, *The Waltz Book* became a kind of musical registry of births, marriages and deaths. In the course of the finished piece, seven birthdays are celebrated (in addition to six actual births) and fifteen of the waltzes might best be thought of as postcards to friends; there are also three 'in memoriam' waltzes, two wedding presents and a love letter. (The fact that, between starting and finishing this work, I had time to meet, fall in love and marry rather underlines the intractability of the compositional task.) In a few of these pieces there are actual attempts to portray the dedicatee in the music, but generally the connection between music, title and dedication is rather more elliptical than that. Sometimes, indeed, I simply happened to find myself writing a waltz on a friend's birthday and so the piece became associated with that person regardless of its musical content.

Largely as a result of the personalisation of the waltzes, musical quotations of various sorts began to crop up and these can be found now, by the assiduous listener, scattered throughout *The Waltz Book*. Eight composers are celebrated in titles or dedications and some aspects of their musical styles are evoked. But there are also two veiled references, one melodic, one harmonic, to Brahms's Lullaby; there are quotations from a couple of old pop songs; and just before the end there's the borrowing of the rhythmic framework of one of Ravel's *Valses nobles et sentimentales*. Most blatantly, there is a folk dance called 'The Whole World Waltz', which comes from Ostrobothnia in the west of Finland. This waltz, in turn, is the subject of a set of variations (the next four waltzes), and eleven waltzes later it turns up as a distant, wistful recollection.

Individual titles allude to all manner of passing fancies. There are lines of poetry, characters from a children's story, plays on people's names and oblique references to incidental facts and figures from the world outside my window. The assembly of the waltzes into a larger whole also, initially, involved such trivia. For example, I began the project while having the good fortune to live in the house that Peggy Glanville-Hicks left to the nation as a 'haven' for composers. It seemed fitting that I should make reference to this in the piece, and so among the earliest waltzes to be completed was

'Peggy's Waltz'. When it came time to begin the jigsaw puzzle of assembly, I made 'Peggy's Waltz' No. 45, simply because that was the number on the front door of her house. Other waltzes took rather longer to find their place in the grand scheme. 'Waltz for Jasper', for instance, was at No. 55 for a while, but ended up at No. 5.

Once twenty (or so) completed waltzes had been allocated their positions, it became far easier to invent the missing pieces. The waltzes formed themselves into clusters and sequences, in the process becoming longer interludes, slow movements, scherzos, all the time helping to shape the contours of my hour of music by providing peaks and troughs. But it also became clear that in addition to finding a general shape for *The Waltz Book*, there had to be a way of bringing some thematic unity to it. The first piece was entitled 'Invocation', the outline of a waltz dimly making itself known through a haze of overtones. It occurred to me that just as in Musorgsky's *Pictures at an Exhibition*, the opening 'Promenade' returns to provide moments of punctuation and listener orientation, so my first number might do the same. Accordingly, 'Invocation' makes six further appearances during the course of the hour, each time very slightly altered and, on the final occasion, briefly invaded by the memory of that Ostrobothnian folk dance.

The other way in which *The Waltz Book* gains some unity is through thematic cross-referencing. At the beginning of the eighth waltz, aptly named 'Epiphany', a theme is stated. Actually it jumps out at the listener, not only because of its jagged, cascading character, but also because alarmingly it isn't in triple time. This theme reappears in various guises throughout the work, sometimes lurking unnoticed deep in the musical texture, sometimes waving to the listener rather obviously. Finally, forty-five minutes after its initial statement, it reaches a climax in 'Statue Waltz' (No. 53) where it seems simultaneously triumphant and frozen in time. This, if you like, is *The Waltz Book*'s motto theme. But there are many other musical motifs and fragments of motifs that surface repeatedly, and most of them result from an exploration of the form of the waltz itself.

The first two notes I composed in 'Waltz for Jasper' formed a chord of a major third, played on the second and third beats of the bar — on the 'pa-pah' of 'oom-pa-pah'. This figure, with its silent downbeat, is the most prominent and common motif in the entire work. It is heard in the first 'Invocation' and in all the subsequent 'Invocations', and it turns up in maybe twenty of the other waltzes.

But if the unity of *The Waltz Book*, given its piecemeal construction, is what the composer is proudest of, it is probably not the feature that first strikes the listener or the performer. Over and above (and around and beneath) this hard-won unity there is enormous diversity. Within a minute you can do many things. A minute might contain hundreds of notes or just a handful. Those notes might be piled densely on top of each other or strung out in a line. A minute-waltz might be very fast or very slow. From moment to moment, then, at the music's surface, *The Waltz Book* is characterised by variety.

There is also variety at the technical level. For while some of these waltzes are so simple that a Grade I student (or indeed the composer) might be able to play them, there are also waltzes at most other degrees of difficulty. Befitting the nature of the commission, and the proud tradition of Schubert, Chopin, Liszt and Ravel, some of the waltzes are properly in the domain of the virtuoso. And one or two, I am delighted to report, gave Ian Munro almost as much of a headache as he gave me.

Learning to Howl (2001)

Nearly all the words in my song cycle *Learning to Howl* are by women. For almost two decades I composed vocal music for male voices: a dozen works for the tenor Gerald English and a music-theatre piece for the baritone Lyndon Terracini. Knowing who will sing or play your music cannot help but shape the nature of what you compose. You take into account the strengths of the performer, their likes (so far as you know them) and their dislikes. You bear in mind the idiosyncrasies that emerge from their performances and the sound that typically they create. Finally finding myself contemplating a female voice, I could only imagine it articulating female points of view, and so you might say that the single most important shaping factor on this piece, even before a note of it was composed, was the soprano Jane Edwards. It was also Jane who mentioned to me that she had particularly enjoyed working in recent months with three musicians —

saxophonist Margery Smith, harpist Marshall McGuire and percussionist Claire Edwardes — though never at the same time. So they became my instrumental trio for this work.

While searching for the words that would make up the texts of the songs I came across the American writer Lorrie Moore, whose work I found immediately arresting and affecting. Near the beginning of her short novel *Who Will Run the Frog Hospital?* is a passage in which the narrator describes a childhood obsession with trying to 'split' her voice so as to produce chords. She goes out into the fields and tries to unleash the crowd of voices within her. 'There must have been pain in me,' she says. 'I wanted to howl and fly and break apart.' The idea of Jane beginning the song cycle by confessing to the audience that she 'wanted ... to splinter [her] throat into harmonies' was very appealing to me. Quite quickly I found I could imagine how she might sing those words. In fact, I heard her speaking the occasional word, the whole first song gradually moving from a conversational, confessional tone towards something bolder and eventually quite ecstatic.

It is hard to overstate the importance to a song cycle of finding the right words. You know when you have them, and in this case Lorrie Moore gave me not only the words of my first song and the title of the whole piece (building on the line 'I wanted to howl'), but also, by implication, the piece's subject and its structure. Any artist will tell you that the best feeling is when a piece begins to make itself, and you, ostensibly its creator, become, or so it seems, more like a bystander. The thought of Lorrie Moore's text half-spoken, half-sung by Jane's voice told me exactly how the rest of the piece should go. If a song cycle begins with words about childhood, the obvious thing to do next is find other words that will take the piece through to the other end of life. There seemed no reason to avoid the obvious: *Learning to Howl* would be a cradle-to-grave piece, or at any rate a sequence of songs progressing from youth to old age, and from innocence to experience. Suitable texts began to arrive thick and fast. The last one came next.

I once met Elizabeth Smart, the Canadian author of *By Grand Central Station I Sat Down and Wept*. I had set some of her poems to music and on the day we met for lunch in 1985 she gave me hand-corrected typed carbon copies of half-a-dozen new poems. One of these was 'A Warning', in which an 'old woman waddles towards love'. I suddenly remembered this poem. It was the perfect point of destination for *Learning to Howl*. And so, having my beginning and my end, I began to assemble the other words that would fill out the main body of the piece.

Following Lorrie Moore's girl confessing she 'wanted to howl', I put a fragment from Sappho in which she tells her listeners (some twenty-six centuries ago) that, for their delight, she will 'sing in a clear voice'. But she doesn't deliver on her promise, or not immediately, for along comes Emily Dickinson to croak, ironically: 'I'm Nobody! Who are you?'

Teenage attitude, at least in my reading of the Dickinson, now gives way to love — idealised, romantic, sexual.

Christina Rossetti's words are marvellously innocent as they celebrate the 'birthday of my life', while there is something inescapably steamy about the images (and their rhythmic repetitions) in a passage from the collection of Finnish folk poetry known as the *Kanteletar*:

> I'd offer him my lips,
> Though death were in his mouth.
> I'd clamber on his back,
> Though his neck were like the grave.

Love, at least in this instance, is followed by regret. A poem by the pianist Ian Munro (one of just two male writers among eight women) seems to allude to a missed opportunity, maybe even betrayal, after which Queen Elizabeth I laments her inability to forget the love she feels for someone she herself has rejected.

> I am and not, I freeze and yet am burned,
> Since from myself another self I turned.

Emily Brontë and Ann Timoney Jenkin both deal in despair, recrimination and self-mockery, before the Lady Pan, in Wang Wei's devastating portrait of her loneliness, descends into something resembling madness.

But *Learning to Howl* is not a tragedy. On the contrary, Elizabeth Smart's 'old woman' arrives in the nick of time, her frail body housing 'a daemon'. Far from being pitiable, she is potentially dangerous, brimming with 'Sixty years' fuel / Of aimed frustration'. Watch out!

To say that a song cycle writes itself once the text is in place is an exaggeration. Even when one feels like a bystander, one isn't really. But the words certainly provide structure, a series of pegs on which to hang the music. In the case of *Learning to Howl*, the structure includes a series of moments in which the music seems to stand still. These all coincide with further fragments from Sappho scattered through the piece. Each of them is like a frozen moment in time, the singer apparently stopped in her tracks as she remembers something from the past ('Once I saw a small girl picking flowers …'). It is as though she is looking at a photograph of her younger self and feeling regret. The music associated with each Sappho fragment is of the same sort, so these moments function like static refrains. Again, it was the words themselves (and their 2600-year-old provenance) that insisted on this musical representation.

With the other vocal settings, I also tried as far as possible to let the music emerge from the poetry. So while the setting of Lorrie Moore's words is rather informal, Emily Dickinson's speechifying is given a more rhetorical feel. A friend remarked to me that he had enjoyed the pastiche in the piece. In fact there isn't any, but what he was referring to was the rather Victorian folkloric of Christina Rossetti's 'The Birthday of My Life' and the fact that the setting of Queen Elizabeth's words resembles a lute song. My friend was right, but the resemblances were entirely unintentional. The music was in the words, I just heard it and released it, and until he pointed out the result, I was quite unaware of what I'd done.

Where I did calculate my music was in the setting of Ian Munro's poem 'A Walk to the Japanese Garden'. Because of the rather serial nature of the poem in which one event or revelation leads, stepwise, to the next, I devised a long melodic line which repeats, and both the voice and the accompanying vibraphone have it, though they are out of step with each other (another illustration, as it were, of the relationship described in the poem). This melody returns, played by all three instruments before and during the Elizabeth Smart song at the end, as though the frustration felt by Smart's old woman is somehow related to the earlier incident in Munro's Japanese garden.

All acts of composition involve both instinct and calculation. The instinct is that moment when something occurs to you — a chord, a sonority, a melodic pattern or, in the case of a song, the discovery of a text — and you immediately know it's right. I suppose this is what most of us mean when we speak of inspiration. Often enough these little epiphanies are completely accidental, the only skill involved is in recognising them for what they are. But the next step is always analytical. The composer — the artist — must pause to ask *why* the chord or melodic pattern seems right. It is not enough to feel it; if one is to make use of the discovery in building a piece, it needs to find its exact place in the overall scheme. And so first it must be inspected from all angles.

For me, composing usually progresses like this, in fits and starts. And yet in describing this process, I have in effect slowed it down so we can observe it. I doubt if many composers work so deliberately or even consciously: finding a chord, recognising it, pausing to analyse it, then placing it carefully in the context of the piece before advancing. It happens much faster than that and, particularly when things are going well, a lot less deliberately. It's like driving. When one learns, one continually thinks about gear changes, about checking mirrors and giving indications — all of it in response to the traffic conditions around one. Experienced drivers do the same, mostly without thinking about it. Nevertheless they do it.

The act of composing music is very difficult to describe, or even, for the composer, to remember after the event. But songs are a bit different. Partly because they employ texts, allowing us to hear the musical responses to those words, songs reveal the workings of the composer's mind that much more clearly. The music, as it were, comments on the text. But in a song the text gives the music a function, and so in a strange way the text also comments on the music — even when the words were written twenty-six centuries earlier.

Manhattan Epiphanies (1994-1999)

Manhattan Epiphanies attempts the impossible. It seeks to translate the work of four visual artists into music for string orchestra. The artists, who all lived in New York in the middle of the twentieth century, are Mark Rothko, Joseph Cornell, Robert Motherwell and Jackson Pollock. With the exception of Cornell, who was not a painter at all, the others were what art critics labelled 'abstract expressionists', and their art has always appealed to me.

There are five movements in *Manhattan Epiphanies* (Rothko gets two, the other artists one each) and they are quite short, ranging from five to maybe eight minutes. What they have in common is the intention of creating music using the same principles the artists used to create images. In the 'Rothko' pieces, for example, rather monolithic slabs of sound drift downwards and upwards (respectively), as though the listener were reading one of the painter's imposing canvases. If you have ever stood next to a Rothko, you will know that what seems, from a distance, to be all of a piece — a slab of sepia, say, on a larger slab of maroon — is actually full of textural detail. These include not only patches of paint that are more or less thickly applied, but also flaws in the canvas and the occasional hairs from the artist's brush. So the slabs of sound in my 'Rothko' movements are made up of rather intricate figurations that, from a musical distance (that is, if you're not really paying attention), can tend to cancel each other out. The orchestra consists of seventeen string players each of whom plays as a soloist. Within each section, all the instruments will have slightly different versions of the same line, producing a cloud or a smudge of sonority, a single big shape. Yet when one listens hard these single big shapes reveal their intricacies, at least momentarily. I hope I've also managed to imbue the music with some of the emotional intensity I find in Rothko's work, though this may well come down to sheer relentlessness, both movements continuing just a little longer than is comfortable.

In some ways, Joseph Cornell was an outsider. In contrast to the cosmopolitan Russian immigrant Rothko, Cornell lived most of his life on Utopia Parkway in the New York borough of Queens, seldom venturing onto the island of Manhattan and never leaving New York state. His art consists of boxes of found objects, like miniature installations. One peers into them and discovers, for instance, a glass eye, some coins and a small stuffed bird in front of an old, torn theatre poster. I decided that the central movement of *Manhattan Epiphanies* should consist of thirteen tiny pieces, each lasting less than a minute and consisting of found musical objects — phrases, chords and rhythms torn, as it were, from other people's music. In the spirit of Cornell I invited members of the Australian Chamber Orchestra (which commissioned *Manhattan Epiphanies*) to contribute some fragments of favourite pieces, rendering the musical objects more 'found' than if I had simply chosen them myself. So phrases from the slow movement of Brahms's F major string quintet alternate with phrases from Webern's Bagatelles for string quartet; fragments of *Brandenburg* concertos are placed alongside bars from the scherzo of Schoenberg's Wind Quintet, Op. 26. Later in the piece some of the players take up toy instruments, also in the spirit of Cornell. Tin-drum rolls introduce the first chords of Rossini's overture to *The Thieving Magpie*, which lead to Messiaen's *Catalogue d'oiseaux* on a toy piano while other members of the orchestra play assorted bird calls. In composing 'Utopia Parkway: 13 Cornell boxes', I did not invent a single note of music. Like Cornell with his boxes, I simply juxtaposed the things I had found.

When I attended the Guggenheim Museum's Robert Motherwell retrospective in 1984 it was the first time I had been in that building, and the architecture impressed me as much as the art. Because Motherwell's art tends to consist of bold abstract shapes, often in bright primary colours, sometimes in blacks and browns, they formed a contrast with the continuous white spiral of Frank Lloyd Wright's building. 'Motherwell at the Guggenheim' is the most ambitious of the five pieces in *Manhattan Epiphanies* because it attempts to capture in its six-minute span not only the entire exhibition but also the space in which it hung. In the Guggenheim, one generally takes the lift to the top of the building and wends one's way down the spiral ramp. Light pours in at the top of the building and my first aim in 'Motherwell at the Guggenheim' was to find an equivalent for this, a sequence of high-pitched chords that seem to glow with an intense white. The solo violin is a visitor to the exhibition and immediately picks up a note from one of these chords and extends it, affected, as it were, by the mood of the building. But as the violin begins its slow descent, the mood changes. The rest of the string orchestra now presents sudden bursts of sometimes quite violent sound that also affect the mood of the soloist, as anyone might be affected by viewing a sequence of images. By the end of the piece the pitch has sunk as low as it can, the initial feeling of floating radiance having given way to dark driving rhythms.

It took me nearly three months to compose this movement and when I was done I quickly realised it was no good. After three days spent tinkering with it, trying to fix the problems, I tore the manuscript up and decided to rewrite the piece from memory. This time I had the whole thing finished in twenty-four hours and was particularly happy with the result (it is still my favourite movement of the five). I was reminded of working on paintings as a child. Sometimes you can overwork an image until it becomes lost. That, I think, is what happened to the first version of 'Motherwell at the Guggenheim'. The second version, though broadly the same piece, had much more flair and also, now that I think of it, the apparent spontaneity of many of Motherwell's own images.

The final movement of *Manhattan Epiphanies* is the only one to take a specific painting and try to represent it in sound. There is something innately musical about Jackson Pollock's *Blue Poles* (1952). Paintings often suggest music. For example, it is hard to look at one of Canaletto's views of Venice and not imagine the music of Vivaldi: that's a straightforward association. Similarly, Picasso's *Guernica* always makes me hear Schoenberg, a response that probably dates back to some old BBC arts documentary. El Greco evokes Monteverdi; Géricault conjures up Berlioz; Roy Lichtenstein suggests early rock-and-roll. This is all historical and fairly obvious. But *Blue Poles* is different. Pollock's canvas always makes me want to play it; or to be precise, it makes me want to play *from* it, because in many ways it resembles a musical score.

What is remarkable about *Blue Poles* is the amount of movement within the painting. There are several factors contributing to this and all of them relate to the music I composed. First, there is the shape of the canvas itself. Because it is wide, like cinemascope, it invites you to read it from left to right. Most paintings do not. And because it is a large canvas, it also invites you to take it in by *walking* past it.

In this, Pollock's painting approaches the condition of music, revealing itself in stages. The famous poles themselves help this approach. On the most obvious level they divide the painting into sections so that the eye passes from one to the next, adding to that sense of movement. And because the poles are neither straight nor vertical, but jagged and evidently about to topple forwards, they contribute to the painting's internal momentum. For me, they have a further function. Those blue poles remind me of bar lines, with complex and brightly coloured melodic strands cavorting across them.

There's a sense in which this painting seems to dance. It is a characteristic that *Blue Poles* shares with plenty of Pollock's other work. The artist moved quickly across the canvas as he dripped his paint. The paint moved more quickly still, Pollock controlling it with the dexterity of a puppeteer manipulating his dolls. All paintings are the result of movement, but Pollock's art continually makes us aware of his movements, of the act of creation — the *action* of creation. But there is another important and paradoxical aspect to *Blue Poles*. For all the movement, for all the cavorting and dancing, this painting can seem suddenly monolithic, like a Rothko. If you stand at a certain distance from the painting — not so close that you can follow the individual lines, not so far away that you can feel the rhythm of the poles — the surface of the canvas turns into a frozen blur. The movement stops; it is a compact disc on pause, and we can start it up again simply by refocusing on the poles or the arabesques of dripped paint.

That is the paradox I tried to explore in my musical translation of *Blue Poles*.

The tangled musical lines are sinewy, agile and demanding of virtuosity. The individual members of the string orchestra are only completely synchronised with each other in two places: at the very beginning of the piece and just before the end. Each time a 'pole' approaches, the players regroup, but the chords that form these musical poles are never quite synchronised either. Remember, Pollock's poles aren't straight. For the main body of the music, the instrumentalists must consciously avoid playing together, even though all the first violins might have the same phrases as each other. Each player has to give a solo performance, detailed, passionate and intense. In an ideal performance of the piece you should be able to walk through the orchestra, pausing to attend to individual strands of music, just as you are able to follow one of Pollock's trails of dripped paint across the canvas. And then you should be able to stand back and experience the blur.

Whether we actually hear Jackson Pollock's *Blue Poles* in my music is a moot point. As I have maintained throughout this book, such precise translation is impossible. But, more pertinently, what is there to translate? Isn't that the point of abstract art? Isn't that what abstract art shares with music, particularly classical music? It is not *about* anything. It is the thing itself. With figurative painting, the spectator will ask, 'What is it? What does it mean?' With this painting the only possible answers to those questions are, 'It's Jackson Pollock's *Blue Poles*. That's what it means.'

Well, how reassuring. How consoling. And, come to think of it, in an age when meaning is so often twisted and spun by advertisers and politicians in order to sell us their fundamentally dishonest views of the world, how refreshing.

Bibliography

Some books and authors mentioned in passing:

Theodor W. Adorno, 'Glosse über Sibelius' (1938), in *Gesammelte Schriften*, Frankfurt, 1982.

W. H. Auden, *Collected Shorter Poems 1927–1957*, London, 1966.

M. D. Calvocoressi, *Musical Taste and How to Form It*, London, 1925.

Daniel M. Grimley (ed.), *Cambridge Companion to Sibelius*, Cambridge, 2004.

J. H. Eliot, *Berlioz*, London, 1938.

Robin Holloway, *On Music: essays and diversions*, Brinkworth, 2003.

Les Murray, *Poems the Size of Postcards*, Potts Point, 2002.

Roger Nichols, *Ravel*, London, 1977.

Charles Rosen, *Beethoven's Piano Sonatas: a short companion*, New Haven, 2002.

Thomas Shapcott, *Selected Poems 1956–1988*, St Lucia, 1978.

Arnold Schoenberg, *Style and Idea*, New York, 1950.

Maynard Solomon, *Beethoven* (2nd edition), New York, 1998.

Maynard Solomon, *Late Beethoven: music, thought, imagination*, Berkeley, 2003.

Richard Taruskin, *Stravinsky and the Russian Traditions*, Oxford, 1996.

Richard Taruskin, *Oxford History of Western Music*, Oxford, 2005.

Donald Tovey, *A Companion to Beethoven's Pianoforte Sonatas*, London, 1931.

Donald Tovey, *Essays on Musical Analysis*, London, 1935–45.

Index